COLLINS
WORLD ATLAS

Collins World Atlas

Collins
An Imprint of HarperCollinsPublishers
77-85 Fulham Palace Road
London W6 8JB

First Published 1986
Second Edition 1991
Third Edition 1993
Fourth Edition 1994

Fifth Edition 1997
Reprinted 1998
Revised 1998
Reprinted 1999 (twice)
Reprinted with changes 2000
Reprinted 2000

Copyright ©HarperCollinsPublishers Ltd 1997
Maps © Bartholomew Ltd 1997

Collins® is a registered trademark of
HarperCollinsPublishers Ltd

Printed in Italy

ISBN 0 00 448592 0

Cover photo: Zefa Pictures

OH10857 Imp 009

Visit the booklover's website
www.fireandwater.com

CONTENTS

SYMBOLS : TIME ZONES *2*

THE WORLD

EUROPE

ASIA

OCEANIA

NORTH AMERICA

SOUTH AMERICA

AFRICA

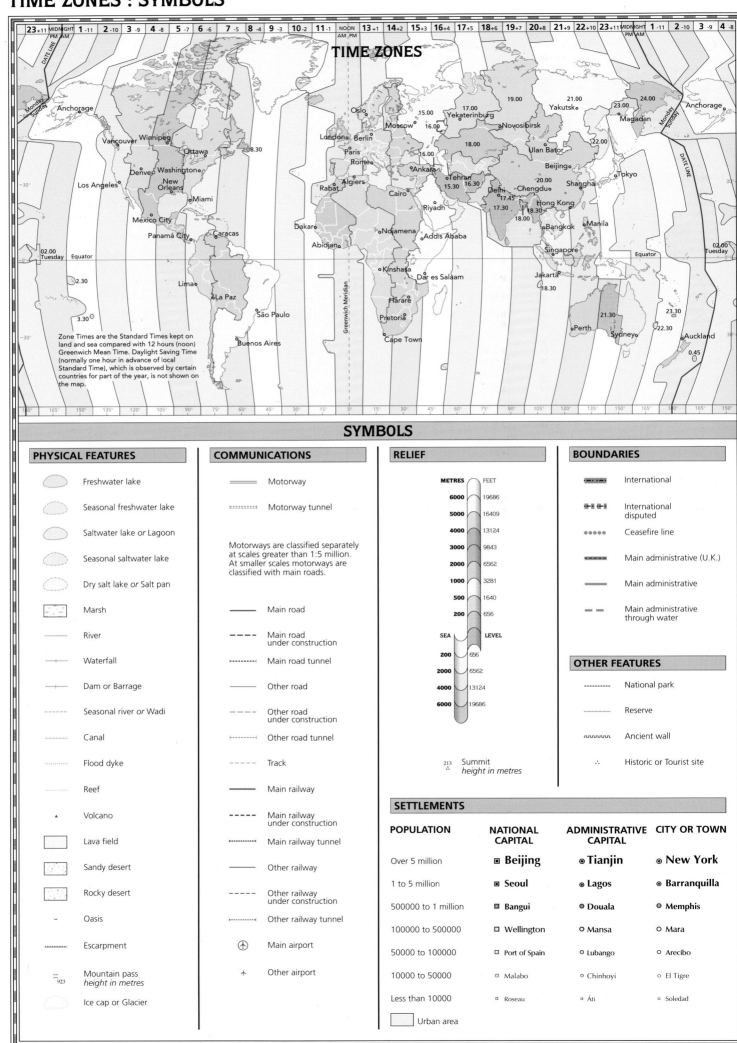

TIME ZONES

| 23 +11 MIDNIGHT PM AM | 1 -11 | 2 -10 | 3 -9 | 4 -8 | 5 -7 | 6 -6 | 7 -5 | 8 -4 | 9 -3 | 10 -2 | 11 -1 | NOON AM ,PM | 13 +1 | 14 +2 | 15 +3 | 16 +4 | 17 +5 | 18 +6 | 19 +7 | 20 +8 | 21 +9 | 22 +10 | 23 +11 MIDNIGHT PM AM | 1 -11 | 2 -10 | 3 -9 | 4 -8 |

Zone Times are the Standard Times kept on land and sea compared with 12 hours (noon) Greenwich Mean Time. Daylight Saving Time (normally one hour in advance of local Standard Time), which is observed by certain countries for part of the year, is not shown on the map.

SYMBOLS

PHYSICAL FEATURES

- Freshwater lake
- Seasonal freshwater lake
- Saltwater lake *or* Lagoon
- Seasonal saltwater lake
- Dry salt lake *or* Salt pan
- Marsh
- River
- Waterfall
- Dam or Barrage
- Seasonal river *or* Wadi
- Canal
- Flood dyke
- Reef
- ▲ Volcano
- Lava field
- Sandy desert
- Rocky desert
- Oasis
- Escarpment
- Mountain pass *height in metres* 923
- Ice cap or Glacier

COMMUNICATIONS

- ══════ Motorway
- ┄┄┄┄ Motorway tunnel

Motorways are classified separately at scales greater than 1:5 million. At smaller scales motorways are classified with main roads.

- ─────── Main road
- ─ ─ ─ ─ Main road under construction
- ┄┄┄┄ Main road tunnel
- ─────── Other road
- ─ ─ ─ ─ Other road under construction
- ┄┄┄┄ Other road tunnel
- ─ ─ ─ Track
- ─────── Main railway
- ─ ─ ─ ─ Main railway under construction
- ┄┄┄┄ Main railway tunnel
- ─────── Other railway
- ─ ─ ─ ─ Other railway under construction
- ┄┄┄┄ Other railway tunnel
- ⊕ Main airport
- ✈ Other airport

RELIEF

METRES	FEET
6000	19686
5000	16409
4000	13124
3000	9843
2000	6562
1000	3281
500	1640
200	656
SEA	LEVEL
200	656
2000	6562
4000	13124
6000	19686

213 △ Summit *height in metres*

BOUNDARIES

- ─·─·─ International
- ┝┷┥ International disputed
- ••••• Ceasefire line
- ─··─ Main administrative (U.K.)
- ─────── Main administrative
- ── ── Main administrative through water

OTHER FEATURES

- ┄┄┄┄ National park
- ⋯⋯⋯ Reserve
- ∿∿∿ Ancient wall
- ∴ Historic or Tourist site

SETTLEMENTS

POPULATION	NATIONAL CAPITAL	ADMINISTRATIVE CAPITAL	CITY OR TOWN
Over 5 million	▣ **Beijing**	◉ **Tianjin**	● **New York**
1 to 5 million	▣ **Seoul**	◉ **Lagos**	● **Barranquilla**
500000 to 1 million	▣ **Bangui**	◎ **Douala**	● **Memphis**
100000 to 500000	▢ Wellington	○ Mansa	○ Mara
50000 to 100000	▫ Port of Spain	○ Lubango	○ Arecibo
10000 to 50000	▫ Malabo	○ Chinhoyi	○ El Tigre
Less than 10000	▫ Roseau	○ Áti	○ Soledad
			▢ Urban area

COUNTRY	AREA		POPULATION	CAPITAL CITY	MAIN LANGUAGES	MAIN RELIGIONS	CURRENCY
	sq km	sq mls					
EUROPE							
ALBANIA	28 748	11 100	3 645 000	Tirana	Albanian (Gheg, Tosk dialects)	Muslim, Greek Orthodox	Lek
ANDORRA	465	180	68 000	Andorra la Vella	Catalan, Spanish, French	R.C.	French franc, Spanish peseta
AUSTRIA	83 855	32 377	8 053 000	Vienna	German, Croatian, Turkish	R.C., Protestant	Schilling
BELARUS	207 600	80 155	10 141 000	Minsk	Belorussian, Russian, Ukrainian	Belorussian Orthodox, R.C.	Rouble
BELGIUM	30 520	11 784	10 113 000	Brussels	Dutch (Flemish), French, German, Italian	R.C., Protestant	Franc
BOSNIA-HERZEGOVINA	51 130	19 741	4 484 000	Sarajevo	Bosnian, Serbian, Croatian	Muslim, Serbian Orthodox, R.C., Protestant	Dinar
BULGARIA	110 994	42 855	8 402 000	Sofia	Bulgarian, Turkish, Romany, Macedonian	Bulgarian Orthodox, Muslim	Lev
CROATIA	56 538	21 829	4 495 000	Zagreb	Croatian, Serbian	R.C., Orthodox, Muslim	Kuna
CZECH REPUBLIC	78 864	30 450	10 331 000	Prague	Czech, Moravian, Slovak	R.C., Protestant	Koruna
DENMARK	43 075	16 631	5 228 000	Copenhagen	Danish	Protestant, R.C.	Krone
ESTONIA	45 200	17 452	1 530 000	Tallinn	Estonian, Russian	Protestant, Russian Orthodox	Kroon
FINLAND	338 145	130 559	5 108 000	Helsinki	Finnish, Swedish	Protestant, Finnish (Greek) Orthodox	Markka
FRANCE	543 965	210 026	58 143 000	Paris	French, French dialects, Arabic, German (Alsatian), Breton	R.C., Protestant, Muslim	Franc
GERMANY	357 868	138 174	81 642 000	Berlin	German, Turkish	Protestant, R.C., Muslim	Mark
GREECE	131 957	50 949	10 458 000	Athens	Greek, Macedonian	Greek Orthodox, Muslim	Drachma
HUNGARY	93 030	35 919	10 225 000	Budapest	Hungarian, Romany, German, Slovak	R.C., Protestant	Forint
ICELAND	102 820	39 699	269 000	Reykjavik	Icelandic	Protestant, R.C.	Króna
ITALY	301 245	116 311	57 187 000	Rome	Italian, Italian dialects	R.C.	Lira
LATVIA	63 700	24 595	2 515 000	Riga	Latvian, Russian	Protestant, R.C., Russian Orthodox	Lat
LIECHTENSTEIN	160	62	31 000	Vaduz	German	R.C., Protestant	Swiss franc
LITHUANIA	65 200	25 174	3 715 000	Vilnius	Lithuanian, Russian, Polish	R.C., Protestant, Russian Orthodox	Litas
LUXEMBOURG	2 586	998	410 000	Luxembourg	Letzeburgish (Luxembourgian), German, French, Portuguese	R.C., Protestant	Franc
MACEDONIA, Former Yugoslav Republic of	25 713	9 928	2 163 000	Skopje	Macedonian, Albanian, Turkish, Romany	Macedonian Orthodox, Muslim, R.C.	Denar
MALTA	316	122	371 000	Valletta	Maltese, English	R.C.	Lira
MOLDOVA	33 700	13 012	4 432 000	Chişinău	Romanian, Russian, Ukrainian, Gagauz	Moldovan Orthodox, Russian Orthodox	Leu
MONACO	2	1	32 000	Monaco	French, Monegasque, Italian	R.C.	French franc
NETHERLANDS	41 526	16 033	15 451 000	Amsterdam	Dutch, Frisian, Turkish, Indonesian languages	R.C., Protestant, Muslim	Guilder
NORWAY	323 878	125 050	4 360 000	Oslo	Norwegian	Protestant, R.C.	Krone
POLAND	312 683	120 728	38 588 000	Warsaw	Polish, German	R.C., Polish Orthodox	Złoty
PORTUGAL	88 940	34 340	10 797 000	Lisbon	Portuguese	R.C., Protestant	Escudo
REPUBLIC OF IRELAND	70 282	27 136	3 582 000	Dublin	English, Irish	R.C., Protestant	Punt
ROMANIA	237 500	91 699	22 680 000	Bucharest	Romanian, Hungarian	Romanian Orthodox, R.C., Protestant	Leu
RUSSIAN FEDERATION	17 075 400	6 592 849	148 141 000	Moscow	Russian, Tatar, Ukrainian, many local languages	Russian Orthodox, Sunni, Muslim, other Christian, Jewish	Rouble
RUSSIAN FEDERATION in Europe	3 955 800	1 527 334	106 918 000				
SAN MARINO	61	24	25 000	San Marino	Italian	R.C.	Italian lira
SLOVAKIA	49 035	18 933	5 364 000	Bratislava	Slovak, Hungarian, Czech	R.C., Protestant, Orthodox	Koruna
SLOVENIA	20 251	7 819	1 984 000	Ljubljana	Slovene, Serbian, Croatian	R.C., Protestant	Tólar
SPAIN	504 782	194 897	39 210 000	Madrid	Spanish, Catalan, Galician, Basque	R.C.	Peseta
SWEDEN	449 964	173 732	8 831 000	Stockholm	Swedish	Protestant, R.C.	Krona
SWITZERLAND	41 293	15 943	7 040 000	Bern	German, French, Italian, Romansch	R.C., Protestant	Franc
UNITED KINGDOM	244 082	94 241	58 258 000	London	English, South Indian languages, Chinese, Welsh, Gaelic	Protestant, R.C., Muslim, Sikh, Hindu, Jewish	Pound
UKRAINE	603 700	233 090	51 639 000	Kiev	Ukrainian, Russian, regional languages	Ukrainian Orthodox, R.C.	Hryvnia
VATICAN CITY	0.44	0.17	1 000		Italian	R.C.	Italian lira
YUGOSLAVIA	102 173	39 449	10 544 000	Belgrade	Serbian, Albanian, Hungarian	Serbian Orthodox, Montenegrin Orthodox, Muslim	Dinar
ASIA							
AFGHANISTAN	652 225	251 825	20 141 000	Kabul	Dari, Pushtu, Uzbek, Turkmen	Muslim	Afghani
ARMENIA	29 800	11 506	3 599 000	Yerevan	Armenian, Azeri, Russian	Arm. Orthodox, R.C., Muslim	Dram
AZERBAIJAN	86 600	33 436	7 499 000	Baku	Azeri, Armenian, Russian, Lezgian	Muslim, Russian and Armenian Orthodox	Manat
BAHRAIN	691	267	586 000	Manama	Arabic, English	Muslim, Christian	Dinar
BANGLADESH	143 998	55 598	120 433 000	Dhaka	Bengali, Bihari, Hindi, English, local languages	Muslim, Hindu, Buddhist, Christian	Taka
BHUTAN	46 620	18 000	1 638 000	Thimphu	Dzongkha, Nepali, Assamese, English	Buddhist, Hindu, Muslim	Ngultrum, Indian rupee
BRUNEI	5 765	2 226	285 000	Bandar Seri Begawan	Malay, English, Chinese	Muslim, Buddhist, Christian	Dollar (Ringgit)
CAMBODIA	181 000	69 884	9 836 000	Phnom Penh	Khmer, Vietnamese	Buddhist, R.C., Muslim	Riel
CHINA	9 560 900	3 691 484	1 221 462 000	Beijing	Chinese, regional languages	Confucian, Taoist, Buddhist, Muslim, R.C.	Yuan
CYPRUS	9 251	3 572	742 000	Nicosia	Greek, Turkish, English	Greek Orthodox, Muslim	Pound
EAST TIMOR	14 874	5 743	857 000	Dili	Portuguese, Tetun, English	Roman Catholic	Rupiah
GEORGIA	69 700	26 911	5 457 000	Tbilisi	Georgian, Russian, Armenian, Azeri, Ossetian, Abkhaz	Georgian & Russian Orthodox, Muslim	Lari
INDIA	3 287 263	1 269 219	935 744 000	New Delhi	Hindi, English, regional languages	Hindu, Muslim, Sikh, Christian, Buddhist, Jain	Rupee
INDONESIA	1 919 445	741 102	194 564 000	Jakarta	Indonesian, local languages	Muslim, Protestant, R.C. Hindu, Buddhist	Rupiah
IRAN	1 648 000	636 296	67 283 000	Tehran	Farsi, Azeri, Kurdish, regional languages	Muslim, Baha'i, Christian, Zoroastrian	Rial
IRAQ	438 317	169 235	20 449 000	Baghdad	Arabic, Kurdish, Turkmen	Muslim, R.C.	Dinar
ISRAEL	20 770	8 019	5 545 000	Jerusalem	Hebrew, Arabic, Yiddish, English	Jewish, Muslim, Christian, Druze	Shekel
JAPAN	377 727	145 841	125 197 000	Tokyo	Japanese	Shintoist, Buddhist, Christian	Yen
JORDAN	89 206	34 443	5 439 000	Amman	Arabic	Muslim, Christian	Dinar

COUNTRY	AREA		POPULATION	CAPITAL CITY	MAIN LANGUAGES	MAIN RELIGIONS	CURRENCY
	sq km	sq mls					
KAZAKSTAN	2 717 300	1 049 155	16 590 000	Astana	Kazakh, Russian, German, Ukrainian, Uzbek, Tatar	Muslim, Russian. Orthodox, Protestant	Tanga
KUWAIT	17 818	6 880	1 691 000	Kuwait	Arabic	Muslim, Christian, Hindu	Dinar
KYRGYZSTAN	198 500	76 641	4 668 000	Bishkek	Kirghiz, Russian, Uzbek	Muslim, Russian Orthodox	Som
LAOS	236 800	91 429	4 882 000	Vientiane	Lao, local languages	Buddhist, trad. beliefs, R.C., Muslim	Kip
LEBANON	10 452	4 036	3 009 000	Beirut	Arabic, French, Armenian	Muslim, Protestant, R.C.	Pound
MALAYSIA	332 965	128 559	20 140 000	Kuala Lumpur	Malay, English, Chinese, Tamil, local languages	Muslim, Buddhist, Hindu, Christian, trad. beliefs	Dollar (Ringgit)
MALDIVES	298	115	254 000	Male	Divehi (Maldivian)	Muslim	Rufiyaa
MONGOLIA	1 565 000	604 250	2 410 000	Ulan Bator	Khalka (Mongolian), Kazakh, local languages	Buddhist, Muslim, trad. beliefs	Tugrik
MYANMAR	676 577	261 228	46 527 000	Yangon	Burmese, Shan, Karen, local languages	Buddhist, Muslim, Protestant, R.C.	Kyat
NEPAL	147 181	56 827	21 918 000	Kathmandu	Nepali, Maithili, Bhojpuri, English, local languages	Hindu, Buddhist, Muslim	Rupee
NORTH KOREA	120 538	46 540	23 917 000	Pyongyang	Korean	Trad. beliefs, Chondoist, Buddhist, Confucian, Taoist	Won
OMAN	271 950	105 000	2 163 000	Muscat	Arabic, Baluchi, Farsi, Swahili, Indian languages	Muslim	Rial
PAKISTAN	803 940	310 403	129 808 000	Islamabad	Urdu, Punjabi, Sindhi, Pushtu, English	Muslim, Christian, Hindu	Rupee
PALAU	497	192	17 000	Koror	Palauan, English	R.C., Protestant, trad.beliefs	US dollar
PHILIPPINES	300 000	115 831	70 267 000	Manila	English, Filipino, Cebuano, local languages	R.C., Aglipayan, Muslim, Protestant	Peso
QATAR	11 437	4 416	551 000	Doha	Arabic, Indian languages	Muslim, Christian, Hindu	Riyal
RUSSIAN FEDERATION	17 075 400	6 592 849	148 141 000	Moscow	Russian, Tatar, Ukrainian, local languages	Russian Orthodox, Muslim, other Christian, Jewish	Rouble
RUSSIAN FEDERATION in Asia	13 119 600	5 065 478	41 223 000				
SAUDI ARABIA	2 200 000	849 425	17 880 000	Riyadh	Arabic	Muslim	Riyal
SINGAPORE	639	247	2 987 000	Singapore	Chinese, English, Malay, Tamil	Buddhist, Taoist, Muslim, Christian, Hindu	Dollar
SOUTH KOREA	99 274	38 330	44 851 000	Seoul	Korean	Buddhist, Protestant, R.C., Confucian, trad. beliefs	Won
SRI LANKA	65 610	25 332	18 354 000	Colombo	Sinhalese, Tamil, English	Buddhist, Hindu, Muslim, R.C.	Rupee
SYRIA	185 180	71 498	14 186 000	Damascus	Arabic, Kurdish, Armenian	Muslim, Christian	Pound
TAIWAN	36 179	13 969	21 211 000	Taipei	Chinese, local languages	Buddhist, Taoist, Confucian, Christian	Dollar
TAJIKISTAN	143 100	55 251	5 836 000	Dushanbe	Tajik, Uzbek, Russian	Muslim	Rouble
THAILAND	513 115	198 115	59 401 000	Bangkok	Thai, Lao, Chinese, Malay, Mon-Khmer languages	Buddhist, Muslim	Baht
TURKEY	779 452	300 948	61 644 000	Ankara	Turkish, Kurdish	Muslim	Lira
TURKMENISTAN	488 100	188 456	4 099 000	Ashkhabad	Turkmen, Russian	Muslim	Manat
UNITED ARAB EMIRATES	77 700	30 000	2 314 000	Abu Dhabi	Arabic, English, Hindi, Urdu, Farsi	Muslim, Christian	Dirham
UZBEKISTAN	447 400	172 742	22 843 000	Tashkent	Uzbek, Russian, Tajik, Kazakh	Muslim, Russian Orthodox	Som
VIETNAM	329 565	127 246	74 545 000	Hanoi	Vietnamese, Thai, Khmer, Chinese, local languages	Buddhist, Taoist, R.C., Cao Dai, Hoa Hao	Dong
YEMEN	527 968	203 850	14 501 000	Sana	Arabic	Muslim	Dinar, Rial

OCEANIA

COUNTRY	AREA		POPULATION	CAPITAL CITY	MAIN LANGUAGES	MAIN RELIGIONS	CURRENCY
AUSTRALIA	7 682 300	2 966 136	18 054 000	Canberra	English, Italian, Greek, Aboriginal languages	Protestant, R.C., Orthodox, Aboriginal beliefs	Dollar
FIJI	18 330	7 077	784 000	Suva	English, Fijian, Hindi	Protestant, Hindu, R.C., Muslim	Dollar
KIRIBATI	717	277	79 000	Bairiki	I-Kiribati (Gilbertese), English	R.C., Protestant, Baha'i, Mormon	Austr. dollar
MARSHALL ISLANDS	181	70	56 000	Dalap-Uliga-Darrit	Marshallese, English	Protestant, R.C.	US dollar
FED. STATES OF MICRONESIA	701	271	105 000	Palikir	English, Trukese, Pohnpeian, local languages	Protestant, R.C.	US dollar
NAURU	21	8	11 000	Yaren	Nauruan, Gilbertese, English	Protestant, R.C.	Austr. dollar
NEW ZEALAND	270 534	104 454	3 542 000	Wellington	English, Maori	Protestant, R.C.	Dollar
PAPUA NEW GUINEA	462 840	178 704	4 074 000	Port Moresby	English, Tok Pisin, local languages	Protestant, R.C., trad. beliefs	Kina
SAMOA	2 831	1 093	171 000	Apia	Samoan, English	Protestant, R.C., Mormon	Tala
SOLOMON ISLANDS	28 370	10 954	378 000	Honiara	English, Solomon Islands Pidgin, local languages	Protestant, R.C.	Dollar
TONGA	748	289	98 000	Nuku'alofa	Tongan, English	Protestant, R.C., Mormon	Pa'anga
TUVALU	25	10	10 000	Fongafale	Tuvaluan, English	Protestant	Dollar
VANUATU	12 190	4 707	169 000	Port-Vila	English, Bislama, French	Protestant, R.C., trad. beliefs	Vatu

NORTH AMERICA

COUNTRY	AREA		POPULATION	CAPITAL CITY	MAIN LANGUAGES	MAIN RELIGIONS	CURRENCY
ANTIGUA & BARBUDA	442	171	66 000	St John's	English, Creole	Protestant, R.C.	E. Carib. dollar
THE BAHAMAS	13 939	5 382	278 000	Nassau	English, Creole, French Creole	Protestant, R.C.	Dollar
BARBADOS	430	166	264 000	Bridgetown	English, Creole (Bajan)	Protestant, R.C.	Dollar
BELIZE	22 965	8 867	217 000	Belmopan	English, Creole, Spanish, Mayan	R.C., Protestant, Hindu	Dollar
CANADA	9 970 610	3 849 653	29 606 000	Ottawa	English, French, Amerindian languages, Inuktitut (Eskimo)	R.C., Protestant, Greek Orthodox, Jewish	Dollar
COSTA RICA	51 100	19 730	3 333 000	San José	Spanish	R.C., Protestant	Colón
CUBA	110 860	42 803	11 041 000	Havana	Spanish	R.C., Protestant	Peso
DOMINICA	750	290	71 000	Roseau	English, French Creole	R.C., Protestant	E. Carib. dollar, Pound, Franc
DOMINICAN REPUBLIC	48 442	18 704	7 915 000	Santo Domingo	Spanish, French Creole	R.C., Protestant	Peso
EL SALVADOR	21 041	8 124	5 768 000	San Salvador	Spanish	R.C., Protestant	Colón
GRENADA	378	146	92 000	St George's	English, Creole	R.C., Protestant	E. Carib. dollar
GUATEMALA	108 890	42 043	10 621 000	Guatemala City	Spanish, Mayan languages	R.C., Protestant	Quetzal
HAITI	27 750	10 714	7 180 000	Port-au-Prince	French, French Creole	R.C., Protestant, Voodoo	Gourde
HONDURAS	112 088	43 277	5 953 000	Tegucigalpa	Spanish, Amerindian languages	R.C., Protestant	Lempira
JAMAICA	10 991	4 244	2 530 000	Kingston	English, Creole	Protestant, R.C., Rastafarian	Dollar
MEXICO	1 972 545	761 604	90 487 000	Mexico City	Spanish, Amerindian languages	R.C., Protestant	Peso
NICARAGUA	130 000	50 193	4 539 000	Managua	Spanish, Amerindian languages	R.C., Protestant	Córdoba
PANAMA	77 082	29 762	2 631 000	Panama City	Spanish, English Creole, Amerindian languages	R.C., Protestant, Muslim, Baha'i	Balboa
ST KITTS-NEVIS	261	101	42 000	Basseterre	English, Creole	Protestant, R.C.	E. Carib. dollar
ST LUCIA	616	238	145 000	Castries	English, French Creole	R.C., Protestant	E. Carib. dollar
ST VINCENT & THE GRENADINES	389	150	111 000	Kingstown	English, Creole	Protestant, R.C.	E. Carib. dollar
TRINIDAD AND TOBAGO	5 130	1 981	1 306 000	Port of Spain	English, Creole, Hindi	R.C., Hindu, Protestant, Muslim	Dollar
USA	9 809 386	3 787 425	263 034 000	Washington	English, Spanish, Amerindian languages	Protestant, R.C., Muslim, Jewish, Mormon	Dollar

COUNTRY	AREA		POPULATION	CAPITAL CITY	MAIN LANGUAGES	MAIN RELIGIONS	CURRENCY
	sq km	sq mls					
SOUTH AMERICA							
ARGENTINA	2 766 889	1 068 302	34 768 000	Buenos Aires	Spanish, Italian, Amerindian languages	R.C., Protestant, Jewish	Peso
BOLIVIA	1 098 581	424 164	7 414 000	La Paz	Spanish, Quechua, Aymara	R.C., Protestant, Baha'i	Boliviano
BRAZIL	8 511 965	3 286 470	155 822 000	Brasília	Portuguese, German, Japanese, Italian, Amerindian languages	R.C., Spiritist, Protestant	Real
CHILE	756 945	292 258	14 210 000	Santiago	Spanish, Amerindian languages	R.C., Protestant	Peso
COLOMBIA	1 141 748	440 831	35 099 000	Bogotá	Spanish, Amerindian languages	R.C., Protestant	Peso
ECUADOR	272 045	105 037	11 460 000	Quito	Spanish, Quechua, Amerind. lang.	R.C., Protestant	Sucre
FRENCH GUIANA	90 000	34 749	147 000	Cayenne	French, French Creole	R.C., Protestant	French franc
GUYANA	214 969	83 000	835 000	Georgetown	English, Creole, Hindi, Amerindian languages	Protestant, Hindu, R.C., Muslim	Dollar
PARAGUAY	406 752	157 048	4 828 000	Asunción	Spanish, Guaraní	R.C., Protestant	Guaraní
PERU	1 285 216	496 225	23 560 000	Lima	Spanish, Quechua, Aymara	R.C., Protestant	Sol
SURINAME	163 820	63 251	423 000	Paramaribo	Dutch, Surinamese, English, Hindi, Javanese	Hindu, R.C., Protestant, Muslim	Guilder
URUGUAY	176 215	68 037	3 186 000	Montevideo	Spanish	R.C., Protestant, Jewish	Peso
VENEZUELA	912 050	352 144	21 644 000	Caracas	Spanish, Amerindian languages	R.C., Protestant	Bolívar
AFRICA							
ALGERIA	2 381 741	919 595	28 548 000	Algiers	Arabic, French, Berber	Muslim, R.C.	Dinar
ANGOLA	1 246 700	481 354	11 072 000	Luanda	Portuguese, local languages	R.C., Protestant, trad. beliefs	Kwanza
BENIN	112 620	43 483	5 561 000	Porto Novo	French, Fon, Yoruba, Adja, local languages	Trad. beliefs, R.C., Muslim	CFA franc
BOTSWANA	581 370	224 468	1 456 000	Gaborone	English, Setswana, Shona, local languages	Trad. beliefs, Protestant, R.C.	Pula
BURKINA	274 200	105 869	10 200 000	Ouagadougou	French, More (Mossi), Fulani, local languages	Trad. beliefs, Muslim, R.C.	CFA franc
BURUNDI	27 835	10 747	5 982 000	Bujumbura	Kirundi (Hutu, Tutsi), French	R.C., trad. beliefs, Protestant, Muslim	Franc
CAMEROON	475 442	183 569	13 277 000	Yaoundé	French, English, Fang, Bamileke, local languages	Trad. beliefs, R.C., Muslim, Protestant	CFA franc
CAPE VERDE	4 033	1 557	392 000	Praia	Portuguese, Portuguese Creole	R.C., Protestant, trad. beliefs	Escudo
C. A. R.	622 436	240 324	3 315 000	Bangui	French, Sango, Banda, Baya, local languages	Protestant, R.C., trad. beliefs, Muslim	CFA franc
CHAD	1 284 000	495 755	6 361 000	Ndjamena	Arabic, French, local languages	Muslim, trad. beliefs, R.C.	CFA franc
COMOROS	1 862	719	653 000	Moroni	Comorian, French, Arabic	Muslim, R.C.	Franc
CONGO	342 000	132 047	2 590 000	Brazzaville	French, Kongo, Monokutuba, local languages	R.C., Protestant, trad. beliefs, Muslim	CFA franc
CONGO, DEM. REP.	2 345 410	905 568	43 901 000	Kinshasa	French, Lingala, Swahili, Kongo, local languages	R.C., Protestant, Muslim, trad. beliefs	Franc
CÔTE D'IVOIRE	322 463	124 504	14 230 000	Yamoussoukro	French, Akan, local languages	Trad. beliefs, Muslim, R.C.	CFA franc
DJIBOUTI	23 200	8 958	577 000	Djibouti	Somali, French, Arabic, Issa, Afar	Muslim, R.C.	Franc
EGYPT	1 000 250	386 199	59 226 000	Cairo	Arabic, French	Muslim, Coptic Christian	Pound
EQUATORIAL GUINEA	28 051	10 831	400 000	Malabo	Spanish, Fang	R.C., trad. beliefs	CFA franc
ERITREA	117 400	45 328	3 531 000	Asmara	Tigrinya, Arabic, Tigre, English	Muslim, Coptic Christian	Ethiopian birr
ETHIOPIA	1 133 880	437 794	56 677 000	Addis Ababa	Amharic, Oromo, local languages	Ethiopian Orthodox, Muslim, trad. beliefs	Birr
GABON	267 667	103 347	1 320 000	Libreville	French, Fang, local languages	R.C., Protestant, trad. beliefs	CFA franc
GAMBIA	11 295	4 361	1 118 000	Banjul	English, Malinke, Fulani, Wolof	Muslim, Protestant	Dalasi
GHANA	238 537	92 100	17 453 000	Accra	English, Hausa, Akan, local languages	Protestant, R.C., Muslim, trad. beliefs	Cedi
GUINEA	245 857	94 926	6 700 000	Conakry	French, Fulani, local languages	Muslim, trad. beliefs, R.C.	Franc
GUINEA-BISSAU	36 125	13 948	1 073 000	Bissau	Portuguese, Portuguese Creole, local languages	Trad. beliefs, Muslim, R.C.	Peso
KENYA	582 646	224 961	30 522 000	Nairobi	Swahili, English, local languages	R.C., Protestant, trad. beliefs	Shilling
LESOTHO	30 355	11 720	2 050 000	Maseru	Sesotho, English, Zulu	R.C., Protestant, trad. beliefs	Loti
LIBERIA	111 369	43 000	2 760 000	Monrovia	English, Creole, local languages	Trad. beliefs, Muslim, Protestant, R.C.	Dollar
LIBYA	1 759 540	679 362	5 407 000	Tripoli	Arabic, Berber	Muslim, R.C.	Dinar
MADAGASCAR	587 041	226 658	14 763 000	Antananarivo	Malagasy, French	Trad. beliefs, R.C., Protestant, Muslim	Franc
MALAWI	118 484	45 747	9 788 000	Lilongwe	English, Chichewa, Lomwe, local languages	Protestant, R.C., trad. beliefs, Muslim	Kwacha
MALI	1 240 140	478 821	10 795 000	Bamako	French, Bambara, local languages	Muslim, trad. beliefs, R.C.	CFA franc
MAURITANIA	1 030 700	397 955	2 284 000	Nouakchott	Arabic, French, local languages	Muslim	Ouguiya
MAURITIUS	2 040	788	1 122 000	Port Louis	English, French Creole, Hindi, Indian languages	Hindu, R.C., Muslim, Protestant	Rupee
MOROCCO	446 550	172 414	27 111 000	Rabat	Arabic, Berber, French, Spanish	Muslim, R.C.	Dirham
MOZAMBIQUE	799 380	308 642	17 423 000	Maputo	Portuguese, Makua, Tsonga, local languages	Trad. beliefs, R.C., Muslim	Metical
NAMIBIA	824 292	318 261	1 540 000	Windhoek	English, Afrikaans, German, Ovambo, local languages	Protestant, R.C.	Dollar
NIGER	1 267 000	489 191	9 151 000	Niamey	French, Hausa, local languages	Muslim, trad. beliefs	CFA franc
NIGERIA	923 768	356 669	111 721 000	Abuja	English, Creole, Hausa, Yoruba, Ibo, Fulani	Muslim, Protestant, R.C., trad. beliefs	Naira
RWANDA	26 338	10 169	7 952 000	Kigali	Kinyarwanda, French, English	R.C., trad. beliefs, Protestant, Muslim	Franc
SAO TOME AND PRINCIPE	964	372	127 000	São Tomé	Portuguese, Portuguese Creole	R.C., Protestant	Dobra
SENEGAL	196 720	75 954	8 347 000	Dakar	French, Wolof, local languages	Muslim, R.C., trad. beliefs	CFA franc
SEYCHELLES	455	176	75 000	Victoria	Seychellois, English	R.C., Protestant	Rupee
SIERRA LEONE	71 740	27 699	4 509 000	Freetown	English, Creole, Mende, Temne, local languages	Trad. beliefs, Muslim, Protestant, R.C.	Leone
SOMALIA	637 657	246 201	9 250 000	Mogadishu	Somali, Arabic	Muslim	Shilling
SOUTH AFRICA	1 219 080	470 689	41 244 000	Pretoria/Cape Town	Afrikaans, English, local languages	Protestant, R.C., Muslim, Hindu	Rand
SUDAN	2 505 813	967 494	28 098 000	Khartoum	Arabic, Dinka, Nubian, Beja, Nuer, local languages	Muslim, trad. beliefs, R.C., Protestant	Dinar
SWAZILAND	17 364	6 704	908 000	Mbabane	Swazi, English	Protestant, R.C., trad. beliefs	Emalangeni
TANZANIA	945 087	364 900	30 337 000	Dodoma	Swahili, English, Nyamwezi, local languages	R.C., Muslim, trad. beliefs, Protestant	Shilling
TOGO	56 785	21 925	4 138 000	Lomé	French, Ewe, Kabre, local languages	Trad. beliefs, R.C., Muslim, Protestant	CFA franc
TUNISIA	164 150	63 379	8 896 000	Tunis	Arabic, French	Muslim	Dinar
UGANDA	241 038	93 065	19 848 000	Kampala	English, Swahili, Luganda, local languages	R.C., Protestant, Muslim, trad. beliefs	Shilling
ZAMBIA	752 614	290 586	9 373 000	Lusaka	English, Bemba, Nyanja, Tonga, local languages	Protestant, R.C., trad. beliefs, Muslim	Kwacha
ZIMBABWE	390 759	150 873	11 526 000	Harare	English, Shona, Ndebele	Protestant, R.C., trad. beliefs	Dollar

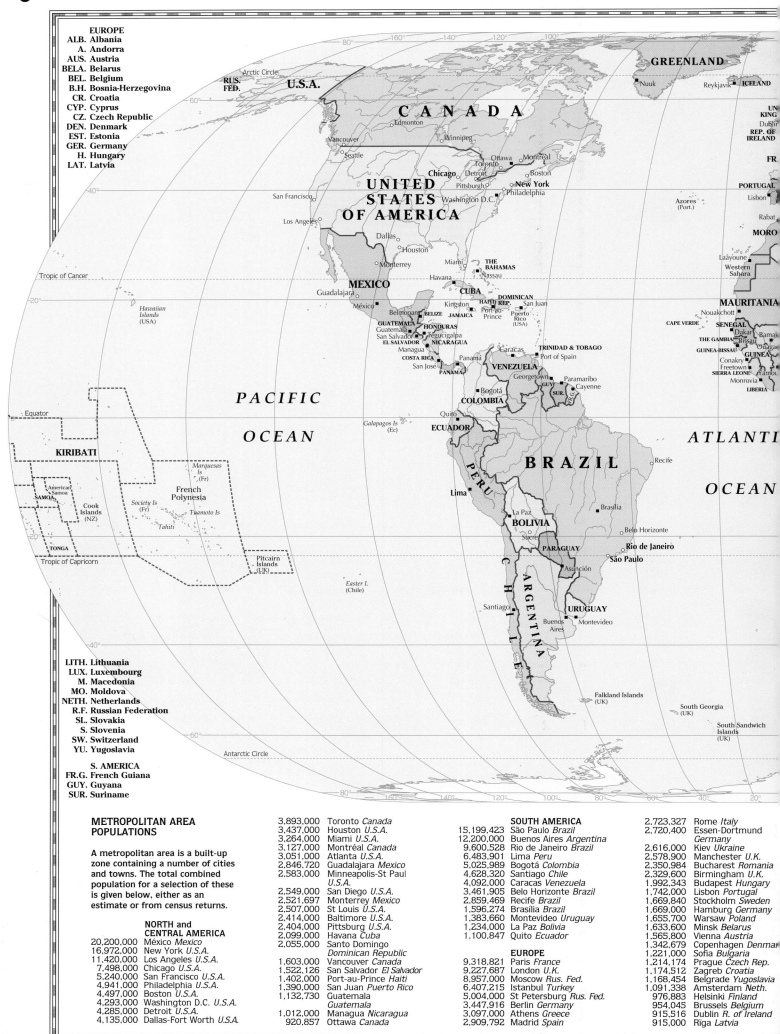

EUROPE
ALB. Albania
A. Andorra
AUS. Austria
BELA. Belarus
BEL. Belgium
B.H. Bosnia-Herzegovina
CR. Croatia
CYP. Cyprus
CZ. Czech Republic
DEN. Denmark
EST. Estonia
GER. Germany
H. Hungary
LAT. Latvia

LITH. Lithuania
LUX. Luxembourg
M. Macedonia
MO. Moldova
NETH. Netherlands
R.F. Russian Federation
SL. Slovakia
S. Slovenia
SW. Switzerland
YU. Yugoslavia

S. AMERICA
FR.G. French Guiana
GUY. Guyana
SUR. Suriname

METROPOLITAN AREA POPULATIONS

A metropolitan area is a built-up zone containing a number of cities and towns. The total combined population for a selection of these is given below, either as an estimate or from census returns.

NORTH and CENTRAL AMERICA

20,200,000	México *Mexico*
16,972,000	New York *U.S.A.*
11,420,000	Los Angeles *U.S.A.*
7,498,000	Chicago *U.S.A.*
5,240,000	San Francisco *U.S.A.*
4,941,000	Philadelphia *U.S.A.*
4,497,000	Boston *U.S.A.*
4,293,000	Washington D.C. *U.S.A.*
4,285,000	Detroit *U.S.A.*
4,135,000	Dallas-Fort Worth *U.S.A.*
3,893,000	Toronto *Canada*
3,437,000	Houston *U.S.A.*
3,264,000	Miami *U.S.A.*
3,127,000	Montréal *Canada*
3,051,000	Atlanta *U.S.A.*
2,846,720	Guadalajara *Mexico*
2,583,000	Minneapolis-St Paul *U.S.A.*
2,549,000	San Diego *U.S.A.*
2,521,697	Monterrey *Mexico*
2,507,000	St Louis *U.S.A.*
2,414,000	Baltimore *U.S.A.*
2,404,000	Pittsburg *U.S.A.*
2,099,000	Havana *Cuba*
2,055,000	Santo Domingo *Dominican Republic*
1,603,000	Vancouver *Canada*
1,522,126	San Salvador *El Salvador*
1,402,000	Port-au-Prince *Haiti*
1,390,000	San Juan *Puerto Rico*
1,132,730	Guatemala *Guatemala*
1,012,000	Managua *Nicaragua*
920,857	Ottawa *Canada*

SOUTH AMERICA

15,199,423	São Paulo *Brazil*
12,200,000	Buenos Aires *Argentina*
9,600,528	Rio de Janeiro *Brazil*
6,483,901	Lima *Peru*
5,025,989	Bogotá *Colombia*
4,628,320	Santiago *Chile*
4,092,000	Caracas *Venezuela*
3,461,905	Belo Horizonte *Brazil*
2,859,469	Recife *Brazil*
1,596,274	Brasília *Brazil*
1,383,660	Montevideo *Uruguay*
1,234,000	La Paz *Bolivia*
1,100,847	Quito *Ecuador*

EUROPE

9,318,821	Paris *France*
9,227,687	London *U.K.*
8,957,000	Moscow *Rus. Fed.*
6,407,215	Istanbul *Turkey*
5,004,000	St Petersburg *Rus. Fed.*
3,447,916	Berlin *Germany*
3,097,000	Athens *Greece*
2,909,792	Madrid *Spain*
2,723,327	Rome *Italy*
2,720,400	Essen-Dortmund *Germany*
2,616,000	Kiev *Ukraine*
2,578,900	Manchester *U.K.*
2,350,984	Bucharest *Romania*
2,329,600	Birmingham *U.K.*
1,992,343	Budapest *Hungary*
1,742,000	Lisbon *Portugal*
1,669,840	Stockholm *Sweden*
1,669,000	Hamburg *Germany*
1,655,700	Warsaw *Poland*
1,633,600	Minsk *Belarus*
1,565,800	Vienna *Austria*
1,342,679	Copenhagen *Denmark*
1,221,000	Sofia *Bulgaria*
1,214,174	Prague *Czech Rep.*
1,174,512	Zagreb *Croatia*
1,168,454	Belgrade *Yugoslavia*
1,091,338	Amsterdam *Neth.*
976,883	Helsinki *Finland*
954,045	Brussels *Belgium*
915,516	Dublin *R. of Ireland*
915,000	Riga *Latvia*

Eckert IV Projection

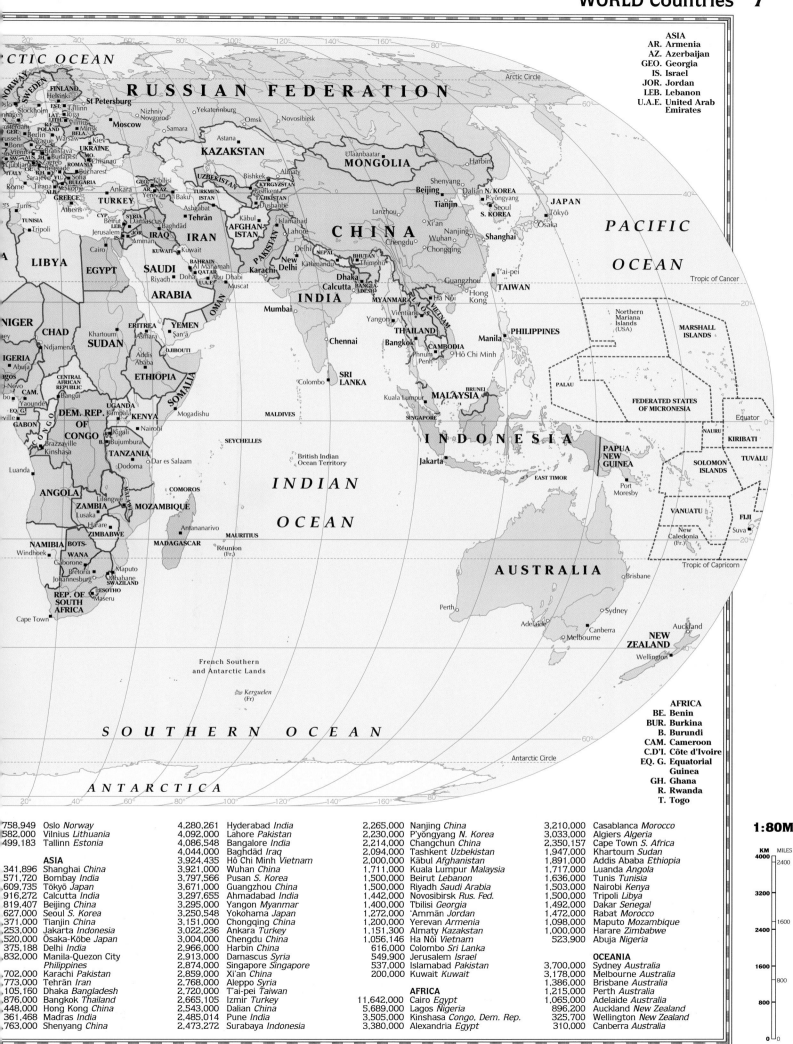

1:80M

KM	MILES
4000	2400
3200	1600
2400	
1600	800
800	
0	0

© Collins

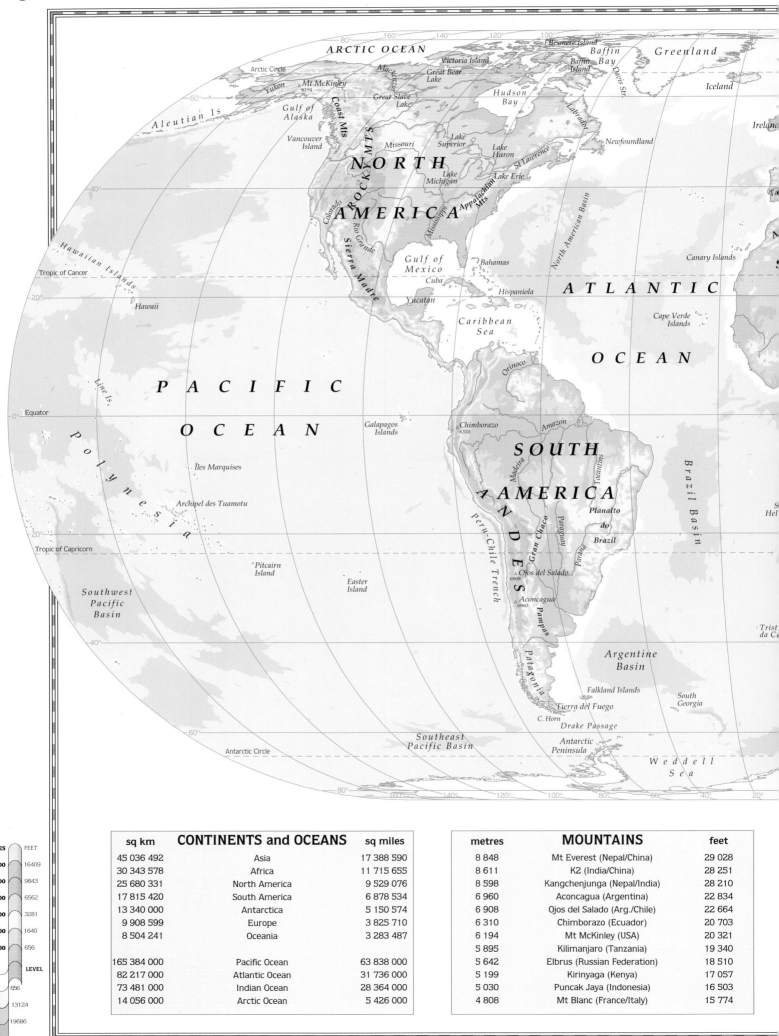

ARCTIC OCEAN

Greenland

Ellesmere Island

Baffin Bay

Baffin Island

Iceland

Arctic Circle

Victoria Island

Great Bear Lake

Mackenzie

Hudson Bay

Davis Str.

Yukon

Mt McKinley 6194

Great Slave Lake

Labrador

Ireland

Aleutian Is

Gulf of Alaska

Coast Mts

Vancouver Island

Missouri

Lake Superior

Lake Huron

St Lawrence

Newfoundland

NORTH

Lake Michigan

Lake Erie

AMERICA

Appalachian Mts

North American Basin

Hawaiian Islands

Tropic of Cancer

Colorado

Rio Grande

Mississippi

Sierra Madre

Gulf of Mexico

Bahamas

Canary Islands

Hawaii

Cuba

ATLANTIC

Yucatan

Hispaniola

Caribbean Sea

Cape Verde Islands

PACIFIC

Orinoco

OCEAN

Line Is

OCEAN

Galapagos Islands

Chimborazo 6310

Amazon

SOUTH

Brazil Basin

Equator

Îles Marquises

Madeira

AMERICA

Tocantins

Polynesia

Archipel des Tuamotu

ANDES

Planalto do Brazil

S. Hel

Peru-Chile Trench

Gran Chaco

Paraguay

Tropic of Capricorn

Pitcairn Island

Easter Island

Ojos del Salado 6908

Paraná

Aconcagua 6960

Pampas

Southwest Pacific Basin

Patagonia

Argentine Basin

Trist da C

Falkland Islands

South Georgia

Tierra del Fuego

C. Horn

Drake Passage

Southeast Pacific Basin

Antarctic Peninsula

Weddell Sea

Antarctic Circle

Eckert IV Projection

METRES	FEET
5000	16409
3000	9843
2000	6562
1000	3281
500	1640
200	656
SEA	LEVEL
200	656
4000	13124
6000	19686

sq km	CONTINENTS and OCEANS	sq miles
45 036 492	Asia	17 388 590
30 343 578	Africa	11 715 655
25 680 331	North America	9 529 076
17 815 420	South America	6 878 534
13 340 000	Antarctica	5 150 574
9 908 599	Europe	3 825 710
8 504 241	Oceania	3 283 487
165 384 000	Pacific Ocean	63 838 000
82 217 000	Atlantic Ocean	31 736 000
73 481 000	Indian Ocean	28 364 000
14 056 000	Arctic Ocean	5 426 000

metres	MOUNTAINS	feet
8 848	Mt Everest (Nepal/China)	29 028
8 611	K2 (India/China)	28 251
8 598	Kangchenjunga (Nepal/India)	28 210
6 960	Aconcagua (Argentina)	22 834
6 908	Ojos del Salado (Arg./Chile)	22 664
6 310	Chimborazo (Ecuador)	20 703
6 194	Mt McKinley (USA)	20 321
5 895	Kilimanjaro (Tanzania)	19 340
5 642	Elbrus (Russian Federation)	18 510
5 199	Kirinyaga (Kenya)	17 057
5 030	Puncak Jaya (Indonesia)	16 503
4 808	Mt Blanc (France/Italy)	15 774

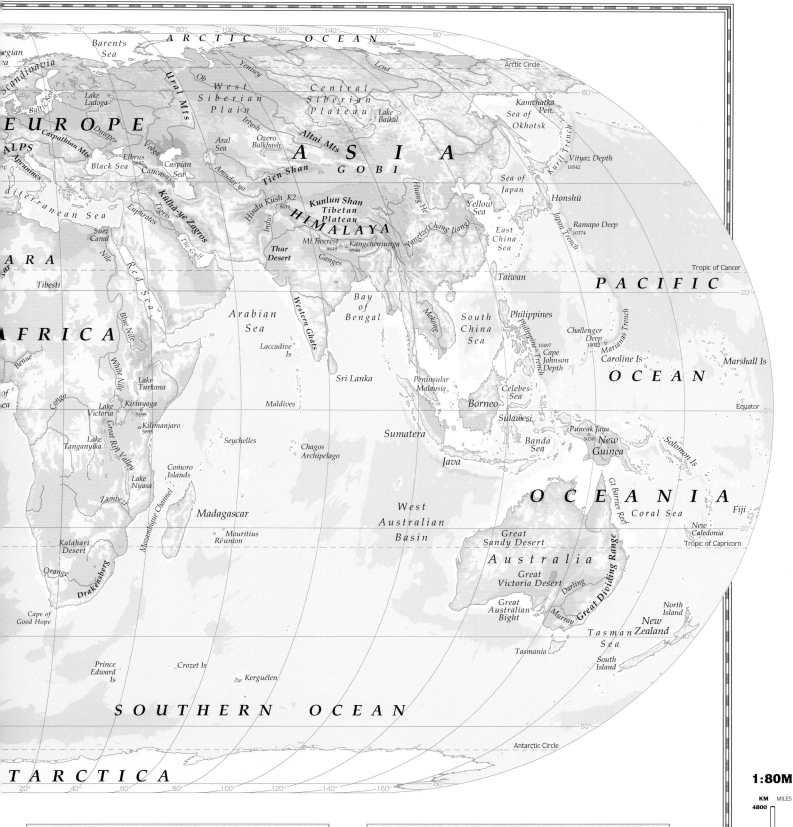

ARCTIC OCEAN

Barents Sea · Scandinavia · Ural Mts · Ob · West Siberian Plain · Irtysh · Yenisey · Central Siberian Plateau · Lena · Arctic Circle · Lake Baikal · Kamchatka Pen. · Sea of Okhotsk

EUROPE · Lake Ladoga · Aral Sea · Altai Mts · A S I A · Kuril Trench · Vityaz Depth 10542

Carpathian Mts · Dnieper · Volga · Ozero Balkhash · G O B I · Sea of Japan

ALPS · Elbrus 5642 · Caspian Sea · Tien Shan · Sea of Japan · Honshū

Apennines · Black Sea · Caucasus · Amudar'ya · Kunlun Shan · Tibetan Plateau · Huang He · Yellow Sea · Ramapo Deep 10374 · Japan Trench

Kühha-ye Zagros · Hindu Kush · K2 8611 · HIMALAYA · Chang Jiang · East China Sea · Tropic of Cancer

Mediterranean Sea · Euphrates · Tigris · Indus · Mt Everest 8848 · Kangchenjunga 8598 · Yangtze · Taiwan · PACIFIC

Suez Canal · The Gulf · Thar Desert · Ganges

Nile · Red Sea · Arabian Sea · Western Ghats · Bay of Bengal · Mekong · South China Sea · Philippines · Challenger Deep 11022 · Marianas Trench

Tibesti

AFRICA · Blue Nile · White Nile · Laccadive Is · Sri Lanka · Peninsular Malaysia · Philippine Trench 10497 · Cape Johnson Depth · Caroline Is · Marshall Is

Benue · Lake Turkana · Kirinyaga 5199 · Maldives · Seychelles · Celebes Sea · OCEAN

Congo · Lake Victoria · Kilimanjaro 5895 · Borneo · Sulawesi · Equator

Lake Tanganyika · Great Rift Valley · Seychelles · Chagos Archipelago · Sumatera · Banda Sea · Puncak Jaya 5030 · New Guinea · Solomon Is

Comoro Islands · Java · New Guinea

Lake Nyasa · Zambezi · West Australian Basin · O C E A N I A · Coral Sea · Fiji

Madagascar · Mauritius · Réunion · Great Sandy Desert · New Caledonia · Tropic of Capricorn

Kalahari Desert · Orange · Mozambique Channel · A u s t r a l i a · Great Dividing Range · North Island

Drakensberg · Great Victoria Desert · Darling · Tasman Sea · New Zealand

Cape of Good Hope · Great Australian Bight · Murray · Tasmania · South Island

Prince Edward Is · Crozet Is · Kerguélen

S O U T H E R N   O C E A N

ANTARCTICA · Antarctic Circle

1:80M

sq km	LAKES	sq miles
371 000	Caspian Sea (Asia)	143 205
83 270	Lake Superior (N. America)	32 140
68 800	Lake Victoria (Africa)	26 560
60 700	Lake Huron (N. America)	23 430
58 020	Lake Michigan (N. America)	22 395
33 640	Aral Sea (Asia)	12 985
32 900	Lake Tanganyika (Africa)	12 700
31 790	Great Bear Lake (N. America)	12 270
30 500	Lake Baikal (Asia)	11 775
28 440	Great Slave Lake (N. America)	10 980
25 680	Lake Erie (N. America)	9 915
22 490	Lake Nyasa (Africa)	8 680

kilometres	RIVERS	miles
6 695	Nile (Africa)	4 160
6 516	Amazon (S. America)	4 048
6 380	Yangtze (Chang Jiang) (Asia)	3 964
6 020	Mississippi-Missouri (N. America)	3 740
5 570	Ob-Irtysh (Asia)	3 461
5 464	Huang He (Asia)	3 395
4 667	Congo (Africa)	2 900
4 425	Mekong (Asia)	2 749
4 416	Amur (Asia)	2 744
4 400	Lena (Asia)	2 734
4 250	Mackenzie (N. America)	2 640
4 090	Yenisey (Asia)	2 541

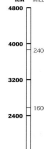

KM MILES
4800
4000 — 2400
3200
2400 — 1600
1600 — 800
800
0 — 0

© Collins

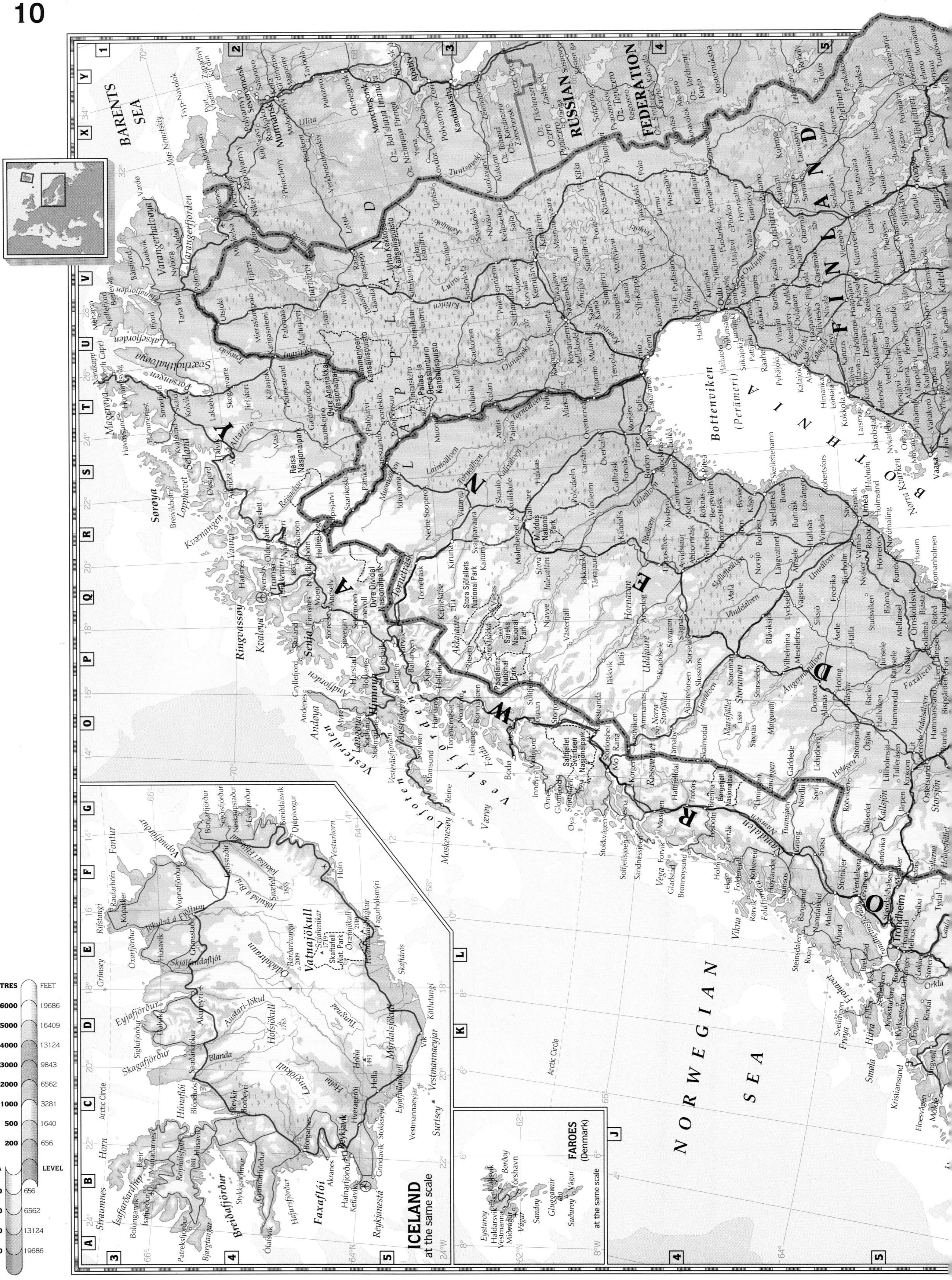

BARENTS SEA

RUSSIAN FEDERATION

FINLAND

LAPLAND

NORWEGIAN SEA

Bottenviken (Perämeri)

Arctic Circle

ICELAND
at the same scale

Vatnajökull

FAROES (Denmark)
at the same scale

METRES	FEET
6000	19686
5000	16409
4000	13124
3000	9843
2000	6562
1000	3281
500	1640
200	656
SEA	LEVEL
200	656
2000	6562
4000	13124
6000	19686

Conic Equidistant Projection

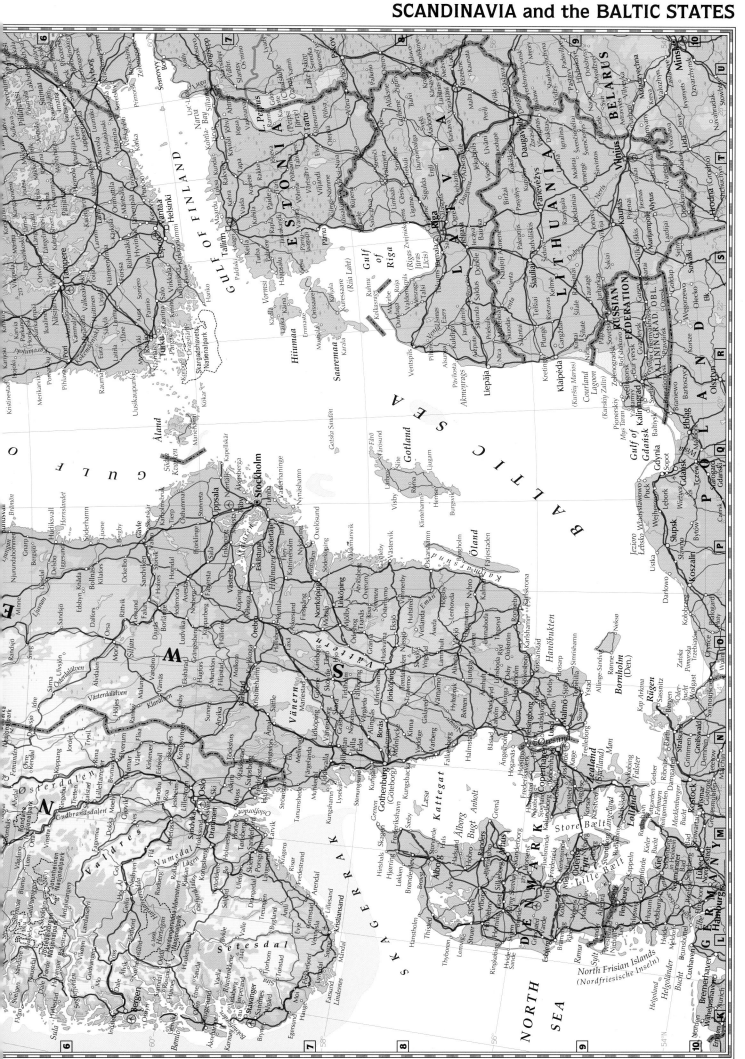

1:5M

KM   MILES

250 — 150

200 — 100

150

100 — 50

50

0 — 0

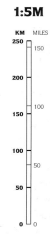

© Collins

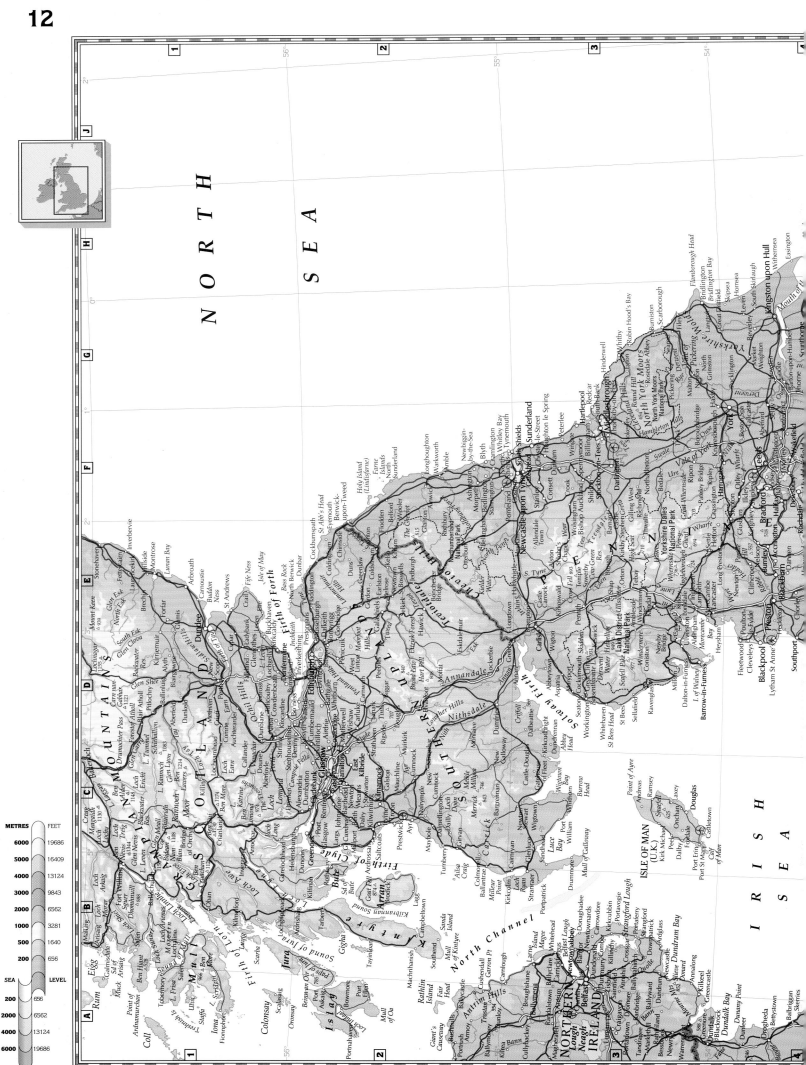

Conic Equidistant Projection

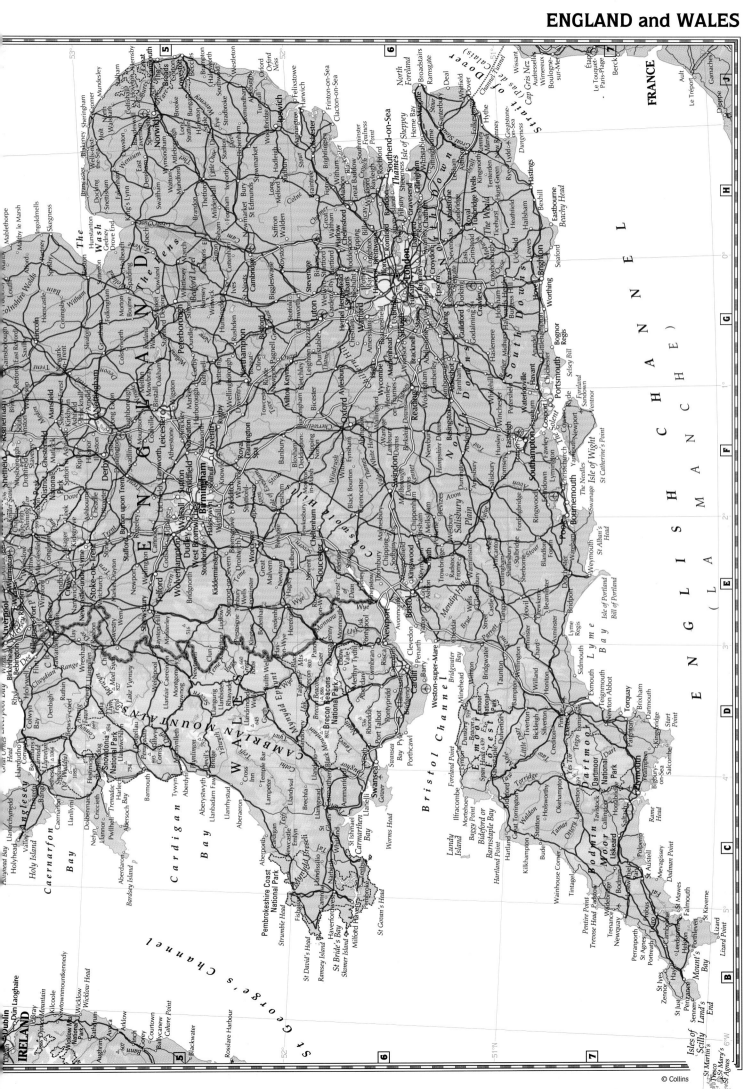

1:2M

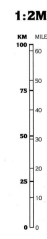

KM   MILES
100   60

                    50

75   40

50   30

                    20

25

            10

0

© Collins

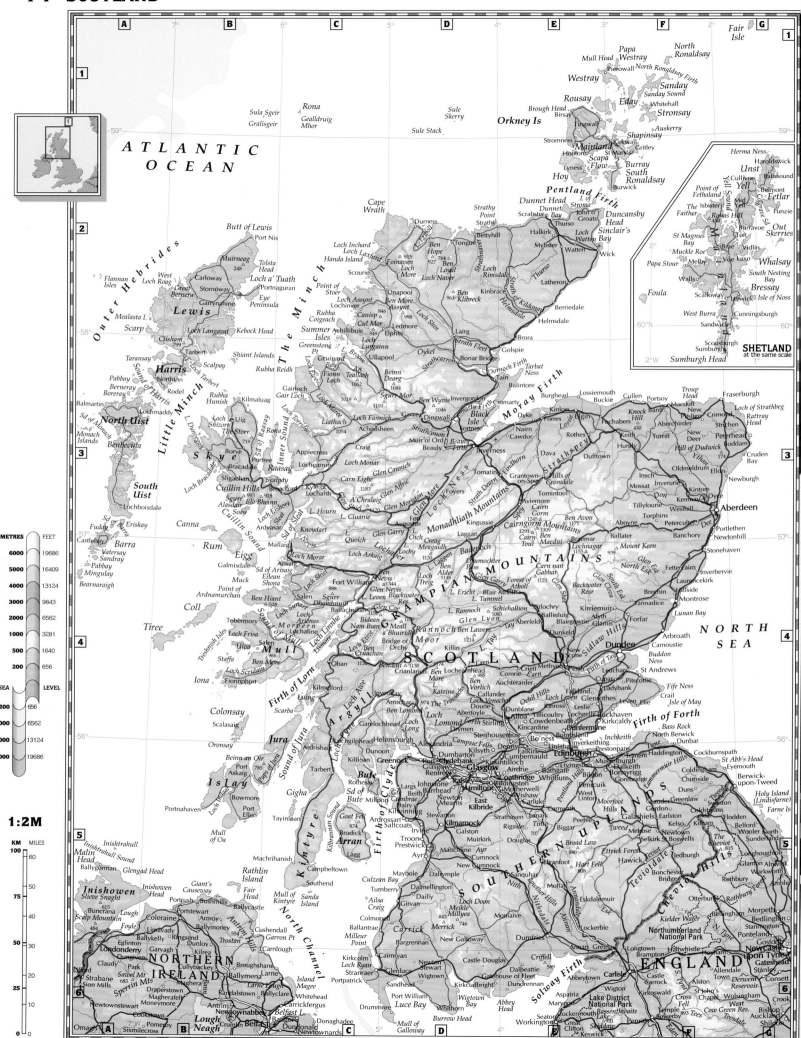

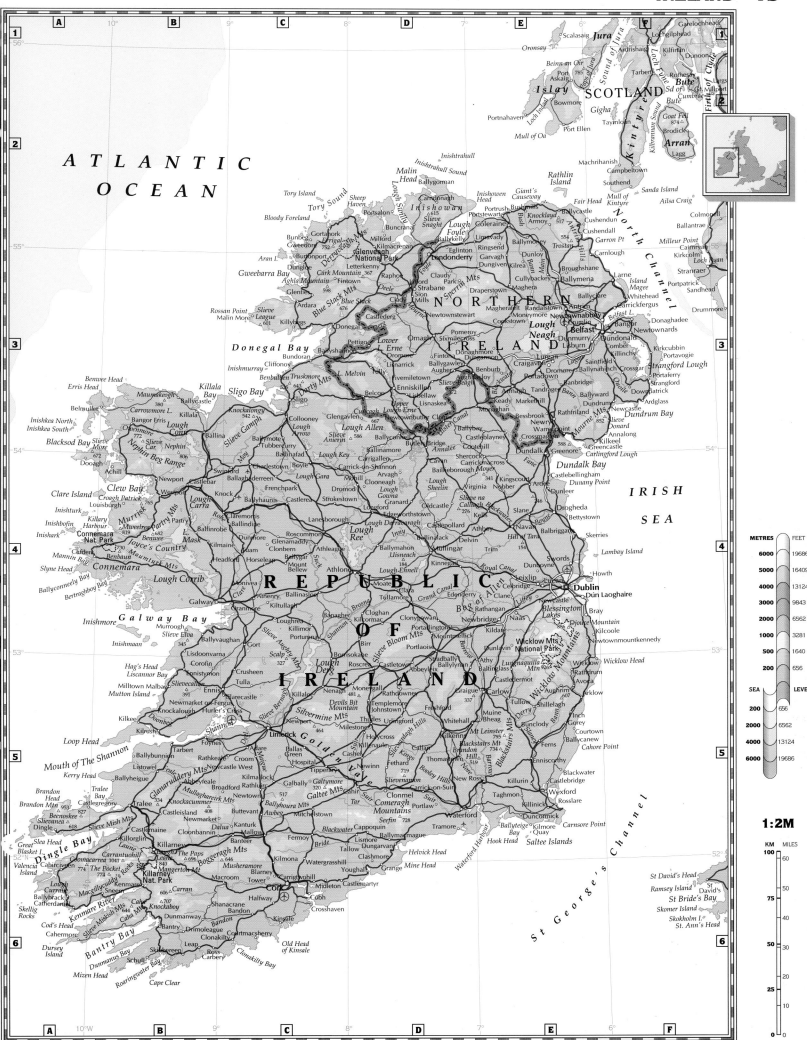

ATLANTIC
OCEAN

SCOTLAND

NORTHERN IRELAND

REPUBLIC
OF
IRELAND

IRISH SEA

METRES	FEET
6000	19686
5000	16409
4000	13124
3000	9843
2000	6562
1000	3281
500	1640
200	656
SEA	LEVEL
200	656
2000	6562
4000	13124
6000	19686

1:2M

KM	MILES
100	60
75	50
	40
50	30
25	20
	10
0	0

Conic Equidistant Projection

© Collins

Conic Equidistant Projection

1:5M

KM MILES 200

300

250 150

200

150 100

100

50

50

0 0

© Collins

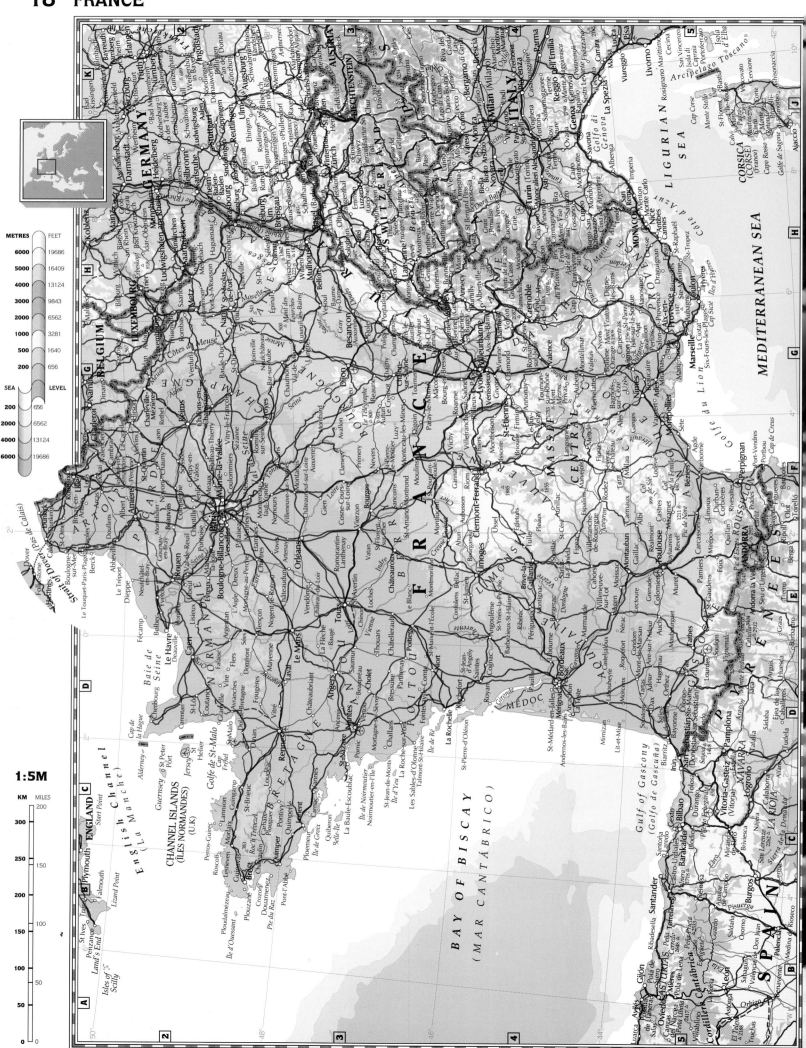

1:5M

Conic Equidistant Projection

© Collins

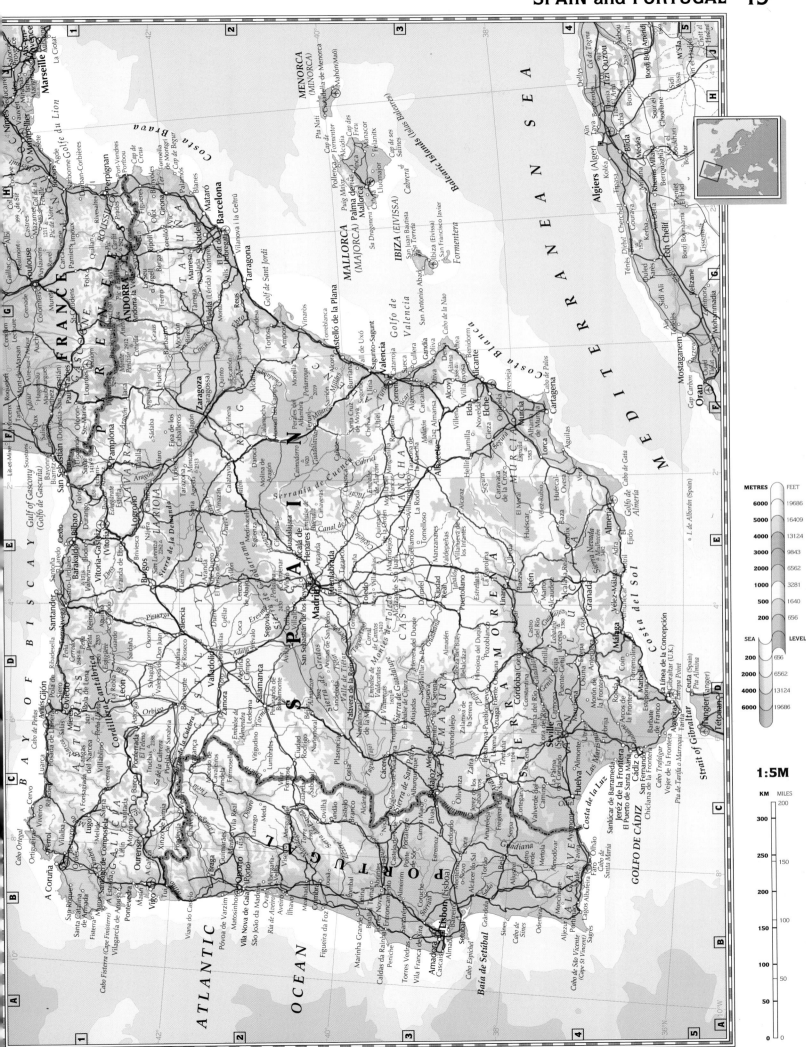

Conic Equidistant Projection

1:5M

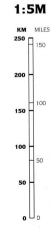

KM	MILES
250	150
200	100
150	
100	50
50	
0	0

© Collins

Divisions of Rus. Fed. not named on map

1. RESP. ADYGEYA (G6)
2. RESP. SEVERNAYA OSETIYA (H7)
3. INGUSHSKAYA RESP. (H7)

1:7M

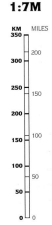

© Collins

Conic Equidistant Projection

METRES | FEET
6000 | 19686
5000 | 16409
4000 | 13124
3000 | 9843
2000 | 6562
1000 | 3281
500 | 1640
200 | 656

SEA | LEVEL

200 | 656
2000 | 6562
4000 | 13124
6000 | 19686

1:21M

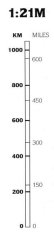

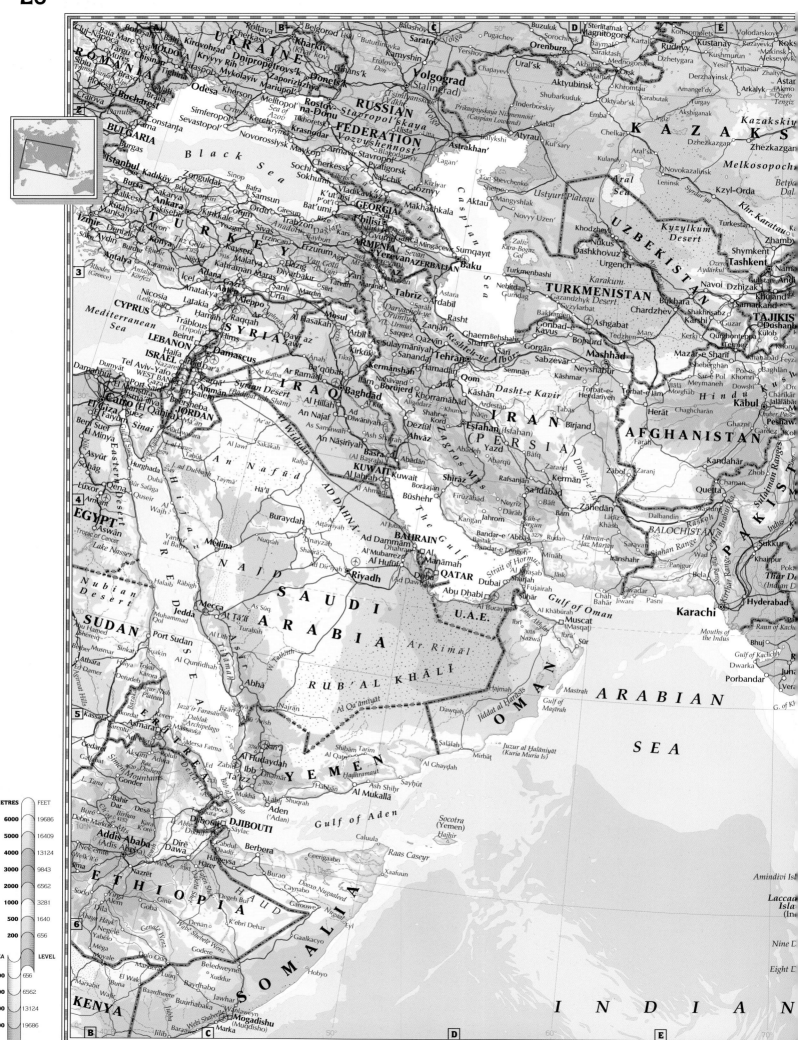

Albers Equal Area Conic Projection

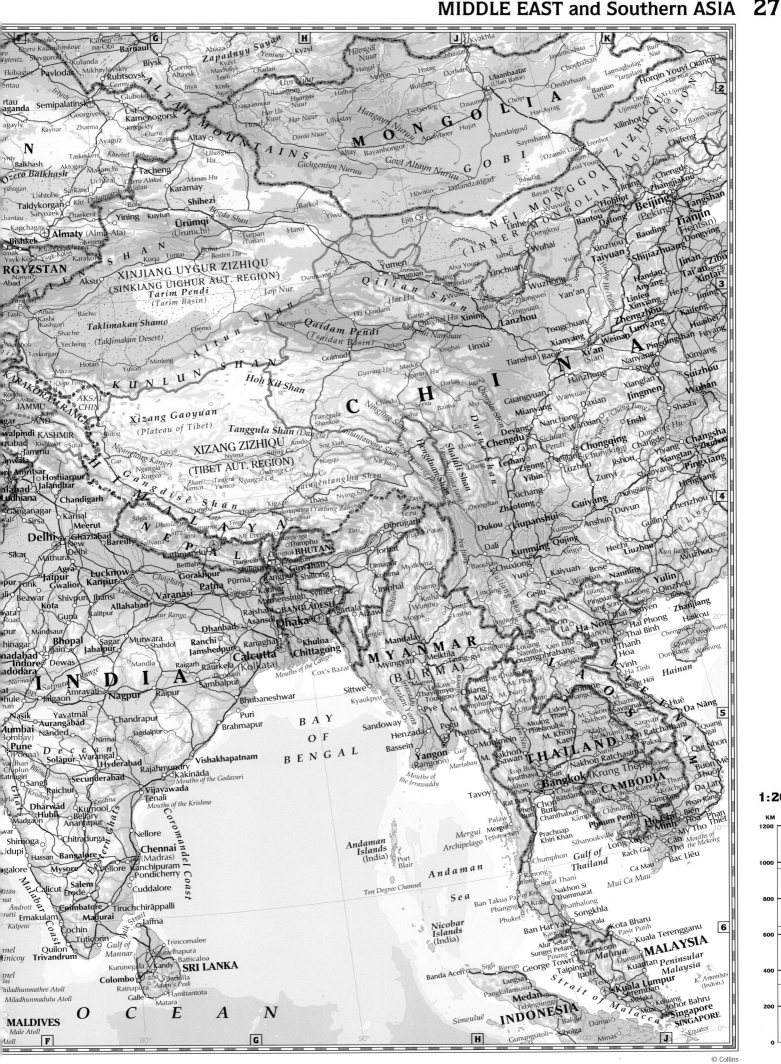

1:20M

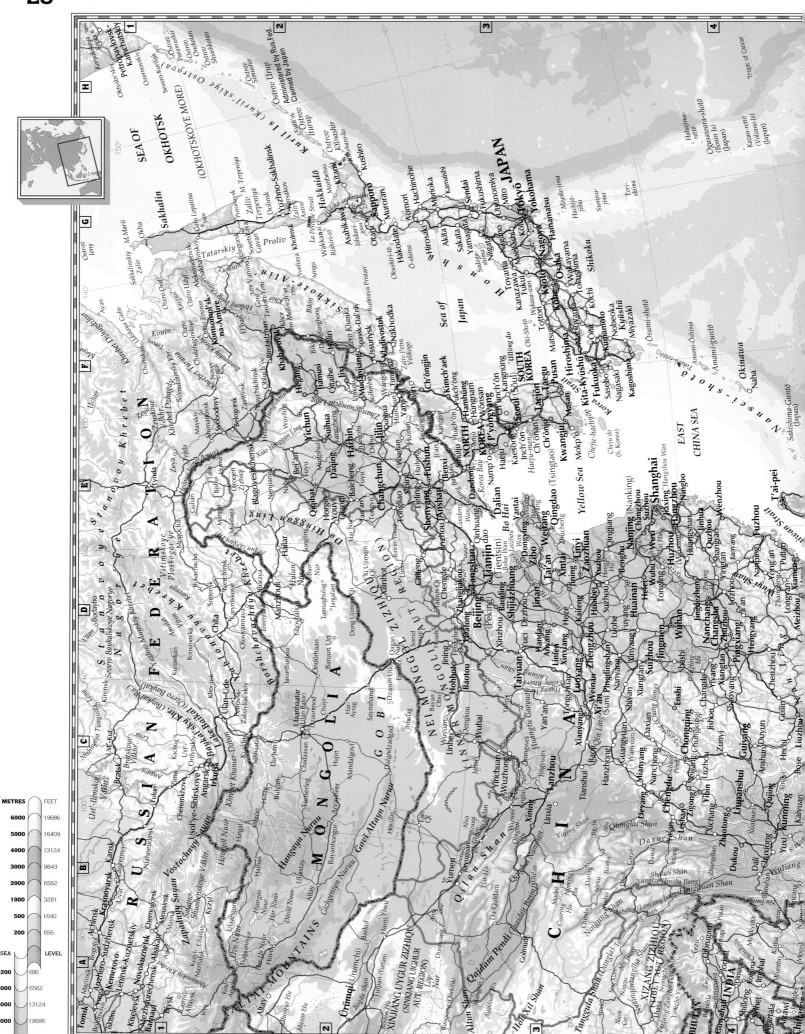

Conic Equidistant Projection

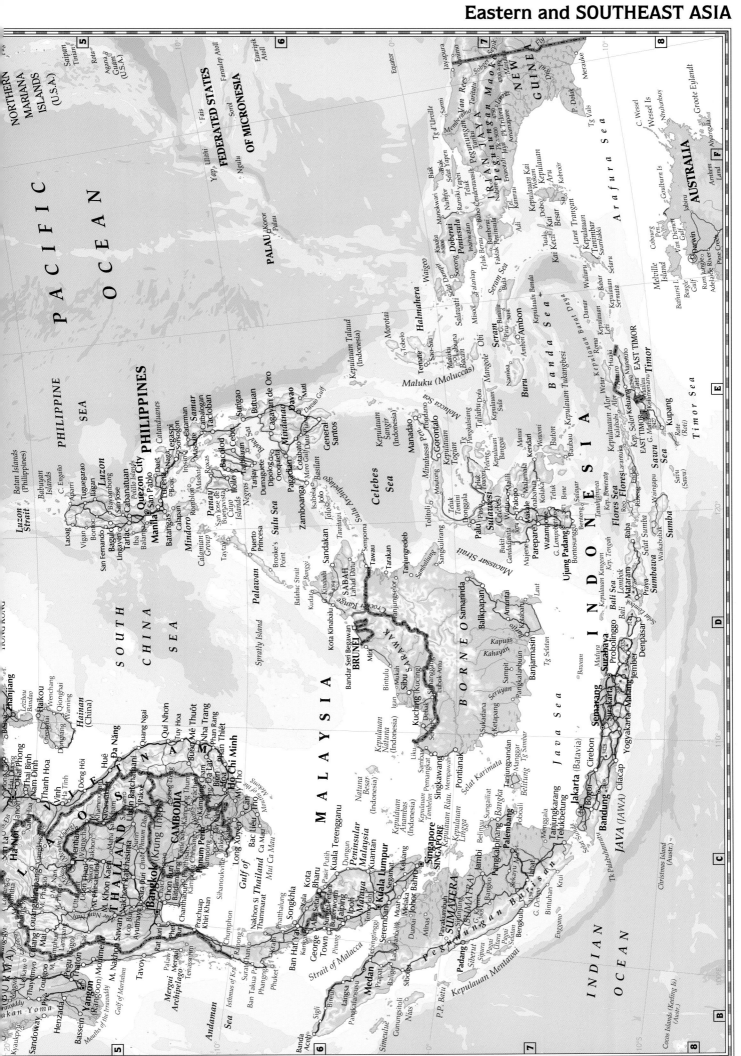

1:20M

KM   MILES

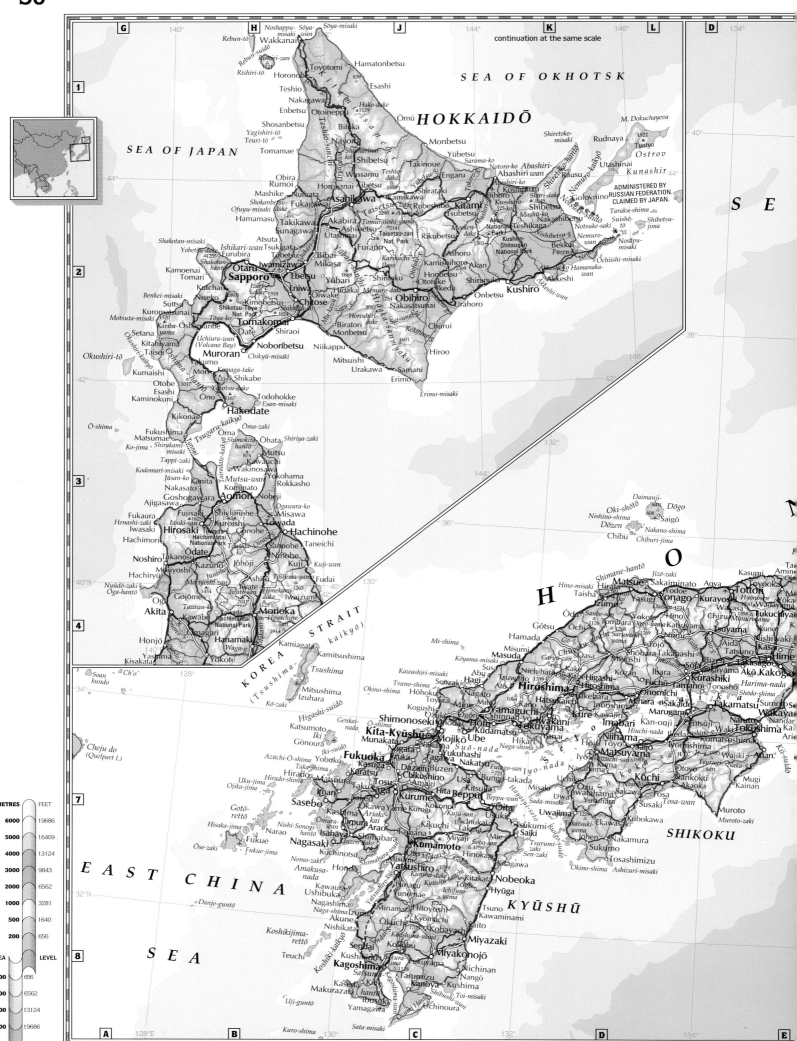

Conic Equidistant Projection

OF JAPAN

S H Ū

S

Tsugaru-kaikyō Ōma-zaki
Shimokita-hantō Ōma Ōhata
Tappi-zaki *874* Mutsu
Kanita Kawauchi Wakinosawa
Kodomari-misaki *Jūsan-ko* *Mutsu-wan* Yokohama
Nakasato Rokkasho
Ajigasawa Shichinohe Misawa
Fukaura **Aomori** Kuroishi **Towada** **Hachinohe**
Fujisaki Gonohe Taneichi
Henashi-zaki *1585* Towada Sannohe
Iwasaki **Hirosaki** Hachimantai Ninohe Kuji
National Park Kuji-wan
Hachimori **Ōdate** Takanosu Kazuno *Jōhōji* Ashiro *Tōshima-yama* Fudai
Noshiro *1263*
Hachiryū Moriyoshi-zan *1454* Iwate-san *125* Himekami-dake
Nyūdō-zaki Gojōme Jūniko *2041* Iwaizumi
Oga-hantō Oga Tazawa-ko **Morioka** Miyako
Akita Kawabe Hachimantai *Hayachine-san* Kawai
National Park *1914* Yamada
Honjō Omagari Yokote **Hanamaki** *Waga-g.* Tōno
Yashima **Kitakami** Esashi *Goyō-zan* Kamaishi
Tobi-shima Kisakata Ogachi *2230* *O-zaki*
Chōkai-san Kurikoma- Mizusawa Ōfunato *Ryōri-zaki*
Sakata Kaneyama *yama* Rikuzen-takata **Kesennuma**
Tsuruoka Shinjō *1628*
Atsumi Obanazawa Ishinoseki
Awa-shima Fuyai Maya-san Gassan Murayama Furukawa Shizugawa **Ishinomaki**
1020 Nishikawa Higashine *Oshika-hantō*
Murakami Asahi-dake Sagae **Yamagata** Tendō *Ishinomaki-* Oshika
Arakawa *1870* Kaminoyama Natori **Sendai** *wan* *Kinka-san*
Nagai *1841* Nanyō Shiroishi Iwanuma
Sadoga-shima Kimpoku-san *1175* Yonezawa Zaō-zan Kakuda
Aikawa *Hime-zaki* Shirone *Iide-san* Sōma
Sawata Ryōtsu **Niigata** Shibata *2105* **Fukushima**
Akadomari Niitsu Kitakata Azuma-san *2024* Haramachi
Sawasaki-bana Ogi Tsubame Gosen Bandai-Asahi Nihonmatsu Namie
Izumozaki Sanjō Kamo Tsugawa Nat. Park **Aizu-wakamatsu** **Kōriyama**
Mitsuke Nishiaizu *1482* Ono Tomioka
Tochio Tadami Inawashiro- Sukagawa
Kashiwazaki Ojiya *1538* Sumon-dake *ko* Ōno Iwaki
Jōetsu Koide Tajima Nasu-dake Shirakawa Shioya-zaki
Nadachi Tōkamachi Kuroiso *1917* Yamizo- Kitaibaraki
Itoigawa Uragawara Muika Mikuni-sammyaku Otawara *yama* Takahagi
Nagano Myōkō-san *2346* Nikkō *1022* Ogawa Hitachi
Heguri-jima Nakano *2446* Nat. Park Ōtawara Yamatsuri
Wajima Iiyama Joshin'etsu Numata Imaichi Utsunomiya
Suzu Shinanomachi *kōgen Nat. Pk* Kasama Hitachi-ōta
Noto Kurobe Jōzu *2578*
Nanao-wan Tate- Suzaka Shibukawa Kanuma **Mito**
Togi *Noto-jima* Himi *yama* Ueda Komoro **Maebashi** Kiryū Moka Shimodate Ishioka
Nanao Shinminato Jōetsu Asama-yama Takasaki Ōta Ishioka Tsuchiura
Takaoka *2702* Asama-yama Kasumiga-ura
Kanazawa Toyama Yarigatake Annaka Isesaki **Ōyama** Abiko Tsukuba
Matto Tonami Kamioka *3180 take* **Matsumoto** Saku Kōnosu Kawagoe Satte
Komatsu Johana Furukawa Haku-san Nirasaki Chichibu-Tama Kumagaya Ageo Narita
Kaga Shirakawa *Haku-san* Takayama Shiojiri Chino *2893* National Park Ōmiya Sakura Chōshi
Kanazu *Nat. Park* Ontake-san Okaya Kōfu Kawaguchi *Inubō-zaki*
Fukui Katsuyama *3063* Suwa Yatsuga- Hachiōji Asaka Funabashi
Ōno *3026* take **Tokyo** Chiba
Sabae Nogohaku-san Gero Ina *Chichibu-Tama Nat. Park* Sagamihara Kawasaki Ichihara
Tateishi- *1617* Kanayama Tsukechi **Matsumoto** Zama Mobara
misaki Imajō Tsukechi Komagane Enzan Fuji-Hakone-Izu Atsugi **Yokohama** Misaki
Ōbama Gifu Kakamigahara Nakatsugawa *2190* Minobu Hadano Yokosuka *Bōsō-* Katsuura
Tsuruga Seki *Ena-san* Fujiyoshida Hiratsuka Kamakura *hantō*
Nagahama Inazawa Tajimi *2191* Hiratsuka Odawara Futtsu Kamogawa
Ōgaki Kasugai Iida *Fuji-Hakone-Izu* **Fuji** Mishima Uraga-suidō Tateyama
Maihara Hashima Kuwana *Nat. Park* Fujinomiya Atami Nat. Park Numazu *Sagami-* Chikura
Hikone Inazawa Tenryū Shimizu *wan* *Suno-saki* *Nojima-zaki*
Moriyama **Nagoya** Kariya Okazaki Shizuoka Numazu *Sagami-nada*
Kusatsu *Ise-wan* Anjō Toyokawa Fujieda **Shizuoka** Izu *Mihara-yama*
Suzuka Tōkai Toyohashi Yaizu Shimada *hantō* *764* Ō-shima
Nara Yokkaichi Tokoname Iwata Hamakita Kakegawa *Suruga-* Higashi-
Ueno Gamagōri **Hamamatsu** *wan* *izu*
Iga Tahara *Mikawa-wan* *Omae-zaki* Shimoda
Sakurai *Irago-* *Irō-zaki*
Kashihara *misaki* Izu-
Ōsaka Matsusaka Ise Toba shotō Nii-jima
Yoshino-Kumano Ise-shima *Daiō-zaki* *Kōzu-shima*
National Park Daiō Miyake-jima

Heguri-jima
Nanatsu-shima

P A C I F I C

shotō Mikura-jima
Ko-jima Hachijō-jima
Aoga-shima

O C E A N

Kashima-
nada

© Collins

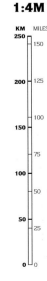

1:4M

KM	MILES
250	150
200	125
	100
150	75
100	50
50	25
0	0

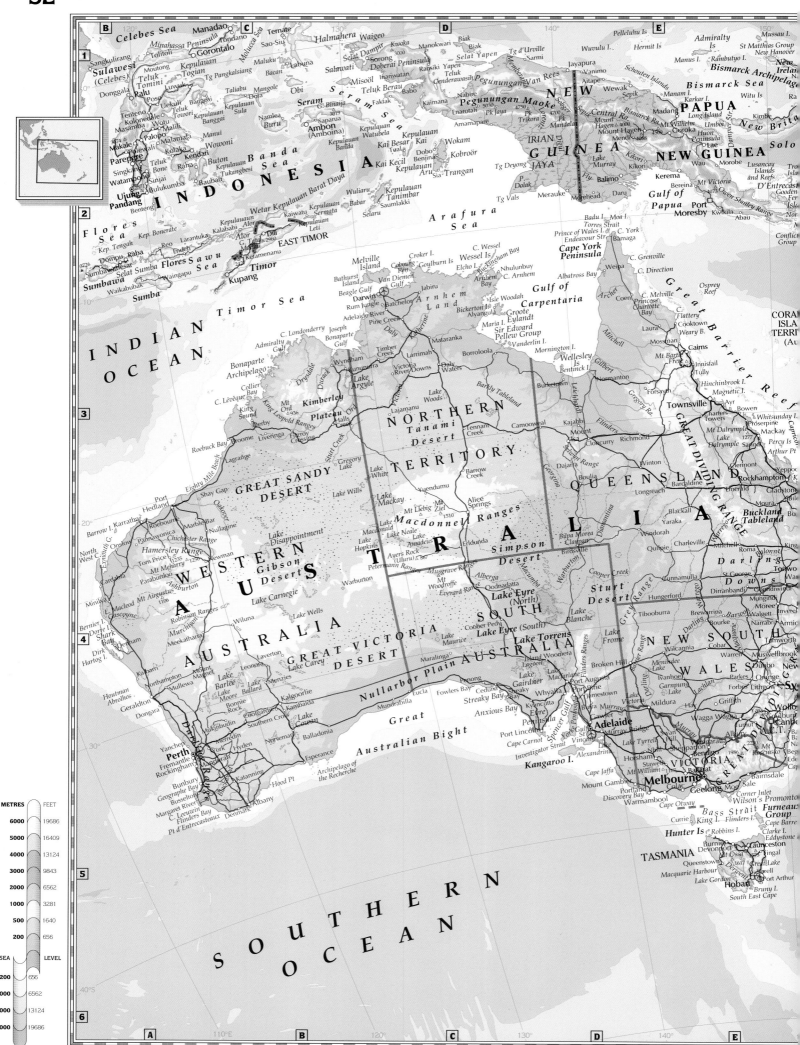

Lambert Azimuthal Equal Area Projection

Map labels

Grid and coordinates: F 160° G Yaren 170° H Arinuka 180° J Equator 0° L

Northern area
Yaren
NAURU
Banaba (Kiribati)
Gilbert Islands (Kiribati)
Nonouti
Tabiteuea
Beru
Nikunau
Onotoa
Kingsmill Group
Tamana
Arorae

KIRIBATI

Howland Island (U.S.A.)
Baker Island (U.S.A.)

Phoenix Islands
McKean Island
Kanton Island
Nikumaroro
Orona (Kiribati)
Manra

Nanumea
Nanumanga
Niutao

TUVALU

Nui
Vaitupu
Nukufetau
Fongafale Funafuti

Nukulaelae

Atafu
Niulakita
Nukunono
Fakaofo

TOKELAU (N.Z.)

Solomon/Coral Sea area
Reef
Nuguria Is
Kilinailau Is
Tauu (Mortlock Is)
Nukumanu Is
George
I.
Bougainville Island
Arawa
Treasury Is
Choiseul
Vella Lavella
Santa Isabel
Kolombangara
Buala
Malu'u
New Georgia Is (Solomon Is)
New Georgia
Rendova
Russell Is
Florida Is
Stewart Is
SOLOMON ISLANDS
Honiara
Maramasike
Guadalcanal
Avuavu
Ulawa I.
San Cristobal
Santa Ana
Kirakira
Rennell
CORAL SEA
Nupani
Swallow Is
Duff Is
Ndeni
Santa Cruz Islands (Solomon Is)
Utupua
Vanikoro Is
Cherry Island
Tikopia Mitre Island

Vanuatu/Fiji area
Torres Islands
Uréparapara
Banks Islands
Vanua Lava
Santa María I.
Espíritu Santo
Tabwémasana 1879
Aoba
Maéwo
VANUATU
Malo
Pentecost I.
Norsup
Ambrym
Malakula
Épi
Émaé
Shepherd Is
Éfaté
Vila
Erromango
Tanna
Aniwa
Futuna
Anatom (Vanuatu)

Rotuma (Fiji)

WALLIS AND FUTUNA IS (Fr.)
Îles Wallis
Îles de Horn

Savaii
SAMOA
Apia
Upolu
Tutuila (U.S.A.)

Niuatoputapu (Tonga)
Tafahi (Tonga)

Yasawa Group
Great Sea Reef
Vanua Levu
Bligh Water
Labasa
Viti Levu
Lautoka
Koro
Suva
Koro Sea
FIJI
Ovalau
Gau
Beqa
Moala
Kadavu Passage
Kadavu
Lakeba
Matuku

Tofua
TONGA

Vava'u Group

Ono-i-Lau (Fiji)
Ata (Tonga)
Tongatapu Group
Nuku'alofa

Niue (N.Z.)

New Caledonia area
Îles Chesterfield (New Caledonia)
Récifs d'Entrecasteaux
I. de Sable
Grand Passage
Îles Bélep
Récif des Français
Grand Récif de Cook
Koumac
Ouvéa
Lifou
Îs Loyauté (Loyalty Is) (Fr.)
Tadine
NEW CALEDONIA (NOUVELLE CALÉDONIE) (Fr.)
Maré
Yaté
Nouméa
Grand Récif du Sud
Î. des Pins

Hunter I. (Fr.)
Conway Reef (Fiji)

Horizon Depth • 10882

South Pacific / Tasman
S O U T H
P A C I F I C
O C E A N

Tropic of Capricorn

Norfolk Island (Aust.)

Lord Howe Island (Aust.)

Macquarie

T A S M A N   S E A

Australia edge (left)
Cape Bay
r Island
borough
ntin
our
olture
sbane
leigh
old Coast
yron Bay
allina
on
s Harbour
ville

New Zealand
Three Kings Is
Cape Maria van Diemen
North Cape
Whangarei
Kaipara Harbour
Takapuna
Auckland
Great Barrier Island
Manukau
Tauranga
Bay of Plenty
NORTH ISLAND
Hamilton
Tokoroa
East Cape
Hikurangi
New Plymouth
North Taranaki Bight
Lake Taupo
Wairoa
Gisborne
Mt Egmont (Mt Taranaki) 2518
Mt Ruapehu 2797
Mahia Peninsula
South Taranaki Bight
Napier
Hawke Bay
Cape Farewell
Wanganui
Hastings
Karamea Bight
Palmerston North
Nelson
Masterton
Westport
Greymouth
Blenheim
Lower Hutt
Wellington
Hokitika
Cook Strait
Cape Palliser
Mt Cook (Mt Aoraki) 3754
Southern Alps
Pegasus Bay
NEW ZEALAND
Mt Aspiring 3033
Christchurch
Lake Pukaki
Banks Peninsula
Mt Christina 3030
Lake Tekapo
Canterbury Bight
Resolution Island
Lake Te Anau
Wanaka
Timaru
Cape Providence
Lake Wakatipu
Oamaru
SOUTH ISLAND
Otago Peninsula
Foveaux Strait
Invercargill
Dunedin
Stewart Island
South West Cape
Snares Is

Chatham Islands (N.Z.)
Pitt I.

Bounty Islands

Auckland Is

Scale
1:20M

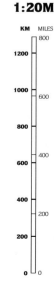

KM   MILES
800
1200
1000   600
800
400
600
400
200
200
0   0

© Collins

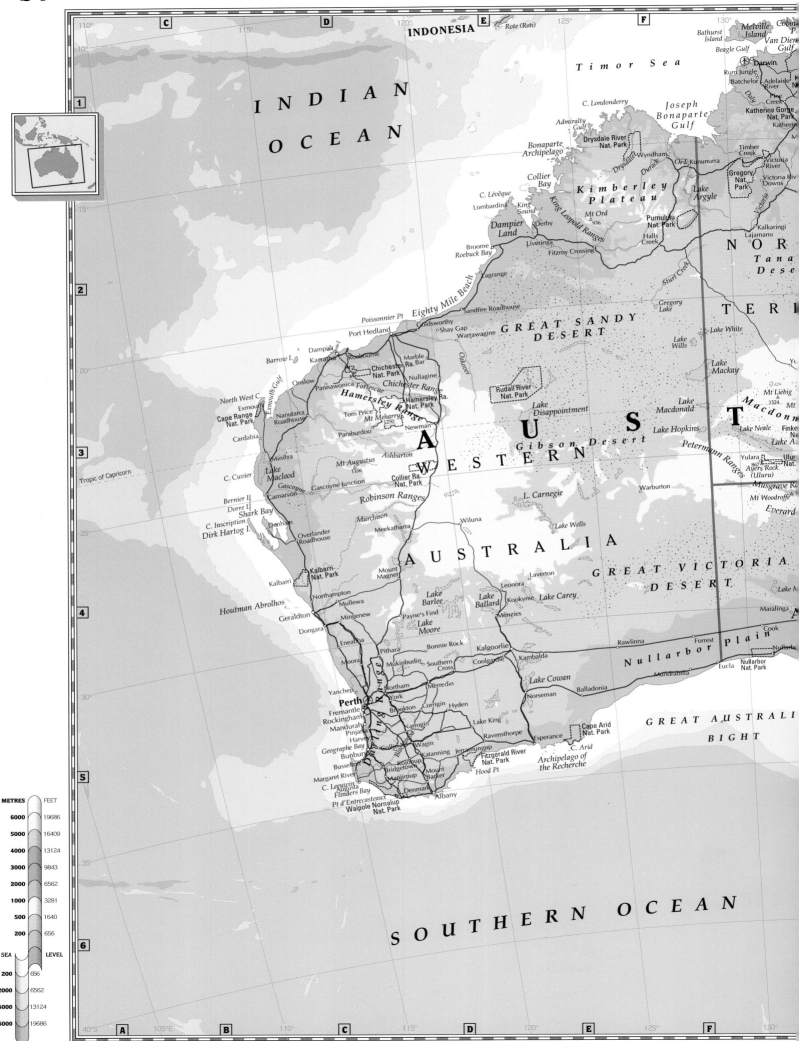

Lambert Azimuthal Equal Area Projection

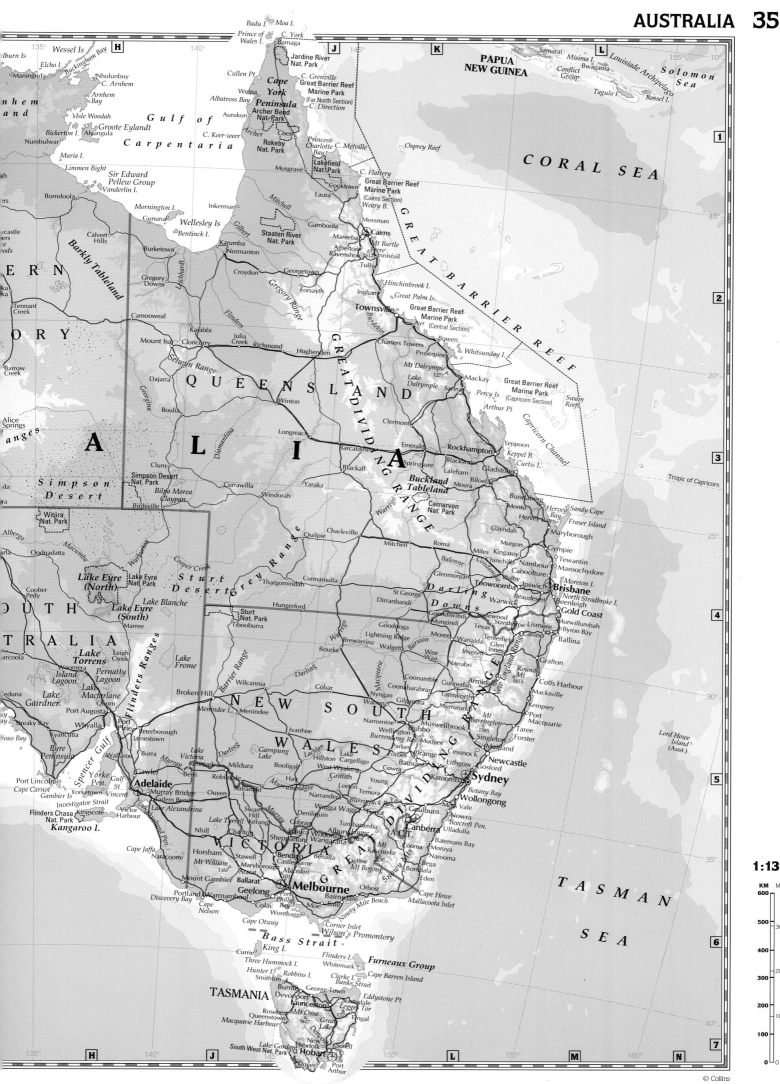

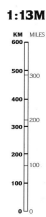

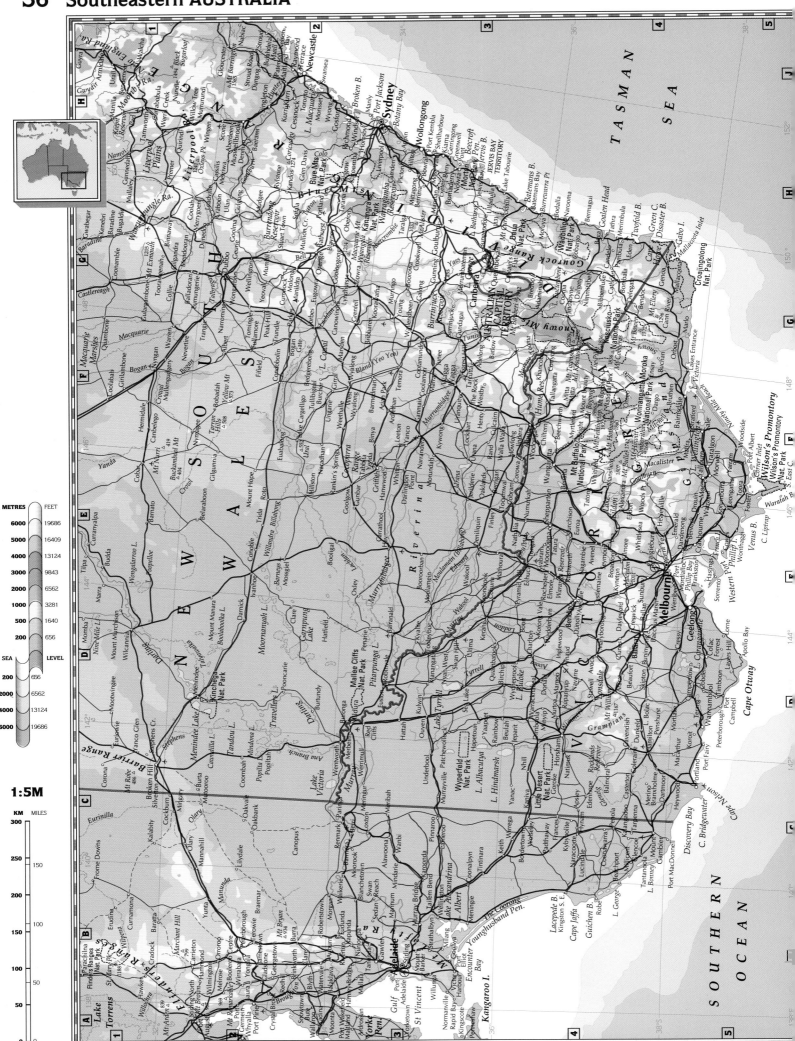

1:5M

Lambert Azimuthal Equal Area Projection

Three Kings Is

Cape Reinga North Cape
Cape Maria van Diemen Te Paki
Parengarenga Harbour
Rangaunu Bay C. Karikari
Awanui Doubtless Bay
Ahipara Bay Kaitaia Kaeo Bay of Islands Cape Brett
Tauroa Pt Ahipara Kerikeri Russell
Broadwood Kawakawa Towai
Poor Knights Is
Hokianga Harbour Kaikohe Whangarei
Mokohinau Is
Donnellys Crossing Bream Bay
Dargaville Maungaturoto Little Barrier
Tangaehe Port Fitzroy
North Head Wellsford Leigh Great Barrier Island
Kaipara Harbour Warkworth Colville Chan.
East Coast Bays Colville Mercury Islands
Takapuna Waiheke I. Coromandel Peninsula
Auckland Onerea Whitianga
Manukau Papakura The Aldermen Is
Manukau Harbour Thames Whangamata
Pukekohe Paeroa Mayor I.
Waiuku Waitakaruru
Port Waikato Bay of Plenty
Glen Afton Huntly Te Aroha Matakana I. Cape Runaway
Ngaruawahia Waihi Katikati Tauranga White I. Hicks Bay
Hamilton Te Puke Whakatane Te Araroa
Cambridge Rotorua East Cape
Kawhia Te Awamutu Ruatoria
Kawhia Harbour Otorohanga Opotiki Tokomaru Bay
Te Kuiti Mangakino Tarawera Mawhai Pt
Awakino Pio Pio Urewera Nat. Park Tolaga Bay
North Taranaki Bight Aria Taupo Gisborne
Mokau Okahukura Murupara Poverty Bay
New Plymouth Waitara Lake Taupo Wairakei
Waitahanui Frasertown
Cape Egmont Whangamomona Turangi Mahia Pen.
Mt Egmont Raetihi Kaimanawa Mts Wairoa
Egmont Nat. Park Tongariro Nat. Park Portland I.
Stratford Mt Ruapehu Ohakune Nuhaka
Opunake Hawke Bay
Hawera Pipiriki Bay View Napier
Patea Taihape Hastings Havelock North
South Taranaki Bight Mangaweka Tikokino C. Kidnappers
Wanganui Apiti Waimarama
Turakina Marton Ongaonga Waipawa
Feilding Dannevirke Waipukurau
Rongotea Woodville Porangahau
Palmerston North Pahiatua Cape Turnagain
Foxton Eketahuna
Levin Castlepoint
Otaki Masterton
Kapiti I. Paraparaumu Upper Hutt Carterton
Porirua Lower Hutt Featherston Flat Point
Wellington Wairarapa Te Wharau
Palliser Bay Martinborough
Cape Palliser

NORTH ISLAND

TASMAN SEA

Cape Farewell Farewell Spit
Collingwood Cape Stephens
Golden Bay D'Urville I.
Kahurangi Pt Separation Pt
Takaka French Pass
Abel Tasman Nat. Park Upper Takaka
Tasman Bay Picton
Karamea Motueka Nelson Blenheim
Mts Richmond Havelock Cloudy Bay
Karamea Bight Wakefield Renwick
Seddonville Hope Saddle Seddon Clifford Bay
Waimangaroa Owen River Cape Campbell
Westport Buller Wairau
Cape Foulwind Murchison Pinnacle
Charleston Inangahua Junction Kekerengu
Reefton Mt Travers Clarence
Runanga Springs Junction Kaikoura
Greymouth Lewis Pass Kaikoura Peninsula
Ahaura Hanmer Springs Oaro
Hokitika L. Brunner Rotomanu L. Sumner Parnassus
Kowhitirangi Waiau Cheviot
Ross Arthur's Pass Culverden Waikari
Abut Head Otira Waipara
Hariharihi Arthur's Pass Nat. Park Oxford Pegasus Bay
Franz Josef Glacier Rangiora Belfast
Fox Glacier Mt Cook Sheffield Kaiapoi
Westland Nat. Park Mt Cook Nat. Park Rolleston Christchurch
Southern Alps Aylesbury Sumner
Te Pirita Banks Peninsula
Haast Canterbury Plains Akaroa
Jackson Head Mayfield Southbridge L. Ellesmere Akaroa Harb.
Cascade Pt Lake Pukaki Ashburton Akaroa
Mt Aspiring Nat. Park Geraldine
Awarua Pt Lake Ohau Temuka Canterbury Bight
Milford Sd Wanaka Timaru
Milford Sound Hawea Pareora
George Sd Queenstown Waimate
Lake Wakatipu Studholme Junction
Fiordland National Park Cromwell Glenavy
Caswell Sd Alexandra Pukeuri Junction C. Wanbrow
Secretary I. Clyde Oamaru
Doubtful Sd Kingston Roxburgh Hampden
Te Anau Middlemarch Moeraki Pt
Lake Te Anau Hyde Shag Pt
Breaksea Sd Mossburn Palmerston
Resolution I. Lumsden Waikouaiti
Dusky Sd Balfour Port Chalmers
Caroline Pt Dipton Mosgiel Otago Peninsula
Providence Gore Dunedin
Chalky Inlet Mataura Brighton
Puysegur Pt Winton Milton
Te Waewae Bay Edendale Balclutha
Riverton Kaitangata
Invercargill Owaka
Foveaux Strait Bluff Nugget Pt
Solander I. Fortrose Long Pt
Codfish I. Chaslands Mistake
Halfmoon Bay Waipapa Pt
Mason B.
Stewart Island
Muttonbird Is Shelter Pt
South West Cape

SOUTH ISLAND

SOUTH PACIFIC OCEAN

Cook Strait

1:5M

c Equidistant Projection © Collins

METRES	FEET
6000	19686
5000	16409
4000	13124
3000	9843
2000	6562
1000	3281
500	1640
200	656
SEA LEVEL	
200	656
2000	6562
4000	13124
6000	19686

KM MILES
300 200
250 150
200 100
150
100 50
0 0

1:17M

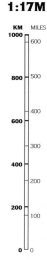

© Collins

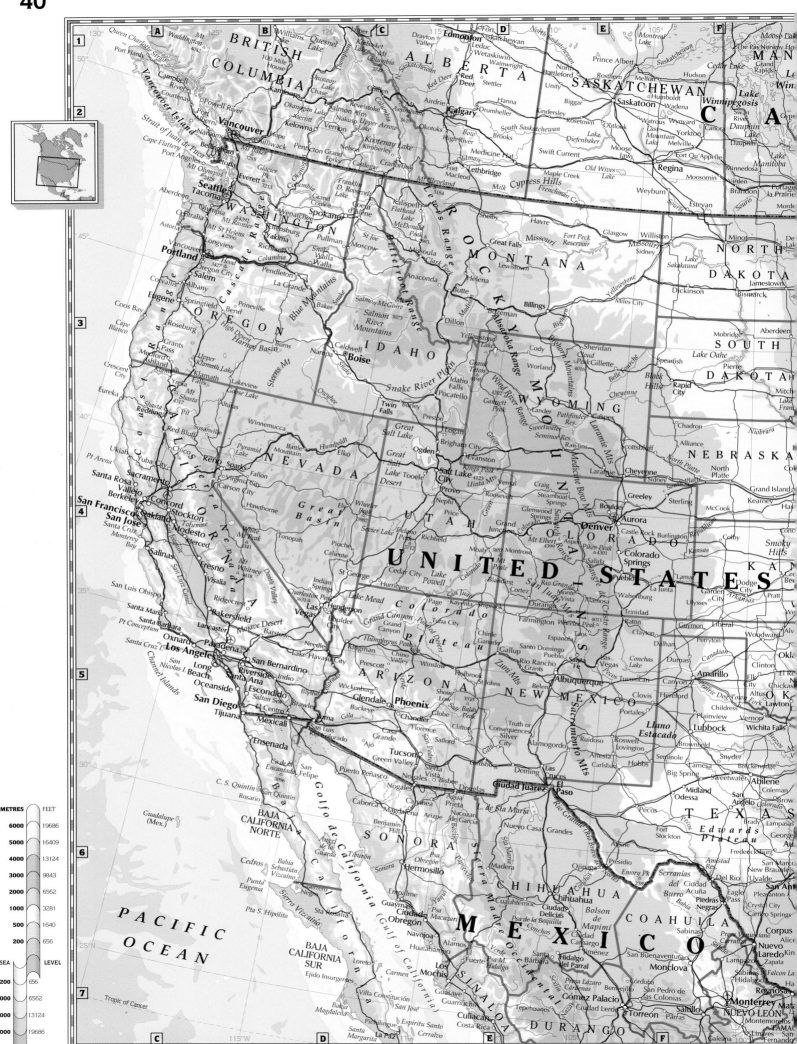

Lambert Conformal Conic Projection

1:12M

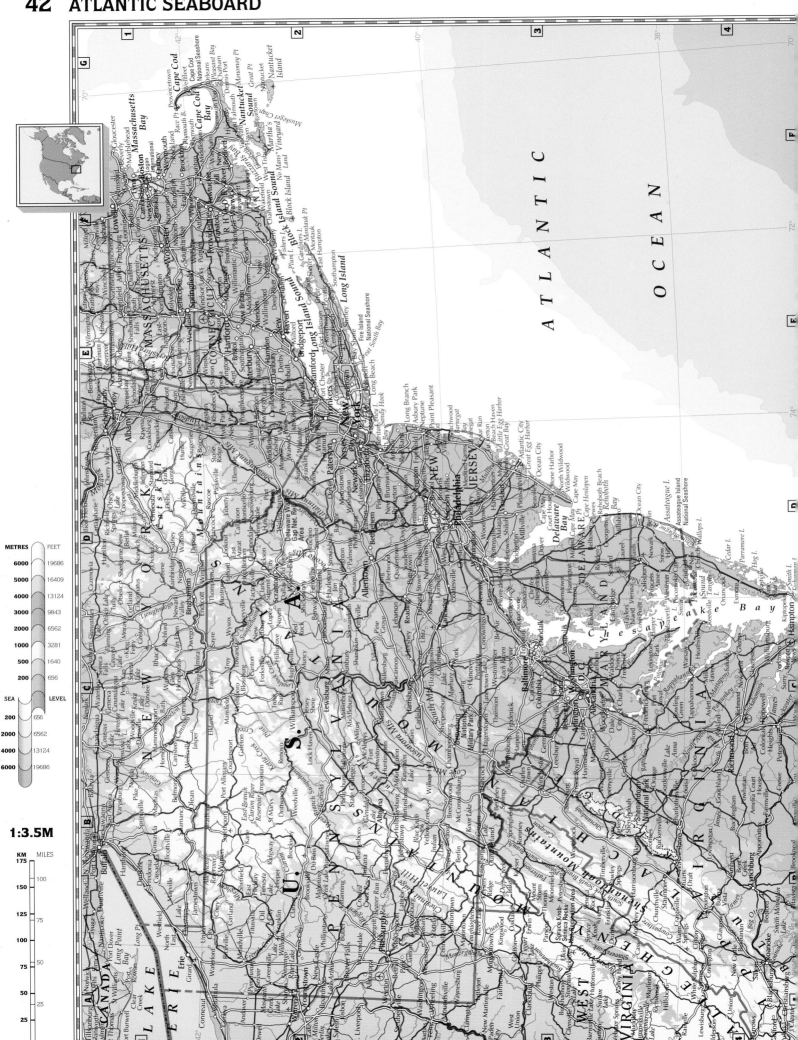

1:3.5M

Lambert Conformal Conic Projection

Lambert Azimuthal Equal Area Projection

ATLANTIC OCEAN

CARIBBEAN SEA

BERMUDA (U.K.)
Hamilton

Tropic of Cancer

THE BAHAMAS

Grand Bahama
Little Abaco
Freeport
Great Abaco
Eleuthera
Governor's Harbour
Nassau
Andros
Cat Island
Exuma Sound
San Salvador (Watling)
Great Exuma
Rum Cay
Long Island
Crooked I. Passage
Crooked Island
Acklins Island
Mayaguana

TURKS AND CAICOS ISLANDS (U.K.)
Caicos Is
Cockburn Town
Turks Is
Matthew Town
Great Inagua

Straits of Florida

Havana (Habana)
Matanzas
Pinar del Rio
Guane
Colón
Santa Clara
Sagua la Grande
Cienfuegos
Caibarién
Placetas
Morón
Sancti Spiritus
Trinidad
Ciego de Avila
Camagüey
Nuevitas
Banes
Victoria de las Tunas
Holguín
Manzanillo
Bayamo
Guantánamo
Santiago de Cuba
Cabo Cruz

CUBA
G. de Batabanó
Isla de la Juventud
Arch. de Sabana
Arch. de Camagüey
Arch. de los Jardines de la Reina
Golfo de Guacanayabo
Sierra Maestra
Pico Turquino 2005

GREAT

CAYMAN ISLANDS (U.K.)
Cayman Brac
Little Cayman
Grand Cayman

JAMAICA
Montego Bay
St Ann's Bay
Savanna la Mar
Mandeville
Kingston
Spanish Town
Jamaica Channel

Swan Islands (Hond.)

HISPANIOLA
Baracoa
Port-de-Paix
Cap-Haïtien
Monte Cristi
Puerto Plata
Santiago
San Francisco de Macorís
Gonaïves
Île de la Gonâve
Pico Duarte 3175
HAITI
Port-au-Prince
DOMINICAN REPUBLIC
La Romana
Santo Domingo
Jérémie
Mt de la Hotte
La Selle
Barahona
Les Cayes
Les Jacmel
Isla Beata
C. Beata

PUERTO RICO (U.S.A.)
Aguadilla
San Juan
Mayagüez
Co de Punta
Ponce
St John
St Croix
Vieques
Isla Mona
Mona Passage

VIRGIN IS (U.K.)
VIRGIN IS (U.S.A.)
Anegada (U.K.)

LEEWARD ISLANDS
ANGUILLA (U.K.)
Saint Martin (Fr.)
St Maarten (Neth.)
St Barthélémy (Fr.)
ANTIGUA AND BARBUDA
St John's
Antigua
Barbuda
ST KITTS-NEVIS
St Eustatius
Basse Terre
Plymouth
MONTSERRAT (U.K.)
GUADELOUPE (Fr.)
Basse Terre
Pointe-à-Pitre
Marie Galante
Roseau
DOMINICA
MARTINIQUE (Fr.)
Fort-de-France

Lesser Antilles

Castries
ST LUCIA

ST VINCENT & THE GRENADINES
Kingstown
Bridgetown
BARBADOS

WINDWARD ISLANDS

GRENADA
St George's
TRINIDAD AND TOBAGO
Tobago
Scarborough
Trinidad
Port of Spain
Arima

NETHERLANDS ANTILLES
Punta Gallinas
ARUBA (Neth.)
Curaçao
Willemstad
Bonaire
I. Orchila (Ven.)
Islas Los Roques (Ven.)
Los Testigos (Ven.)
I. de Margarita (Ven.)
Porlamar
Cumaná
Carúpano
I. La Tortuga (Ven.)
I. Blanquilla (Ven.)
Guiria

Península de la Guajira
Ríohacha
Punto Fijo
G. de Venezuela
Coro
San Juan de los Cayos
Maracaibo
Churuguara
Mene de Mauroa
Puerto Cabello
Barquisimeto
Caracas
Maiquetía
Los Teques
Barcelona
Maracay
Valencia
San Felipe
Rosario
Cabimas
L. de Maracaibo
San Carlos
San Juan de los Morros
Maturín
Tucupita
Boca de Macareo
Caripito
Guanipa
Upata

Santa Marta
Sierra Nevada de Santa Marta
Pico Cristóbal Colón 5775
Parque Nacional Sierra Nevada de Santa Marta
Barranquilla
Cartagena
Calamar
Valledupar
Machiques
Trujillo
Valera
Mérida
Pico Bolívar
Cord. de Mérida
Acarigua
El Baúl
Calabozo
Zaraza
Valle de la Pascua
El Tigre
Ciudad Guayana
Ciudad Bolívar
Upata

Plato
El Banco
Mompós
Lora
San Carlos del Zulia
Barinas
Parque Nacional Aguaro-Guariquito
Orinoco
Embalse de Guri
El Callao
El Dorado

Sincelejo
Montería
Golfo del Darién
Golfo de Morrosquillo

Turbo
Caucasia
Yarumal
Pamplona
Arauca
Guasdualito
San Fernando de Apure
Cabruta
Maripa
La Paragua

PANAMA
Panamá Canal
Panamá
La Chorrera
Aguadulce
Chitré
G. de Panamá
Las Tablas
Península de Azuero
Pta Mala
Punta Mariato
I. de Coiba
Bocas del Toro
Golfo de los Mosquitos
Colón
Santiago
David
Volcán Barú 3475
Golfo de Chiriquí
Isla Coiba

COSTA RICA
Alajuela
San José
Cartago
Limón
Chirripó 3819
G. de Nicoya
Bahía de Coronado
Pen. de Osa
Pta Burica
Puerto Armuelles
Bocas del Toro

NICARAGUA
Siquia
Mico
Bluefields
Lago de Nicaragua
Bonanza
Prinzapolca
Puerto Cabezas
Cayos Miskitos (Nic.)
Is del Maíz (Corn Is) (Nic.)
Isla de Providencia (Col.)
Isla de San Andrés (Col.)

Laguna de Caratasca
Coco
Pta Isabela
Río Grande
Pta de Perlas

MOSQUITIA

COLOMBIA
Quibdó
Cabo Corrientes
Golfo de Cupica
I. de Malpelo (Col.)
Buenaventura
Cali
Palmira
Tuluá
Buga
Sevilla
Cartago
Pereira
Manizales
Armenia
Ibagué
Medellín
Chinquinquira
Honda
Nevado del Ruiz
Neiva
Bogotá
Villavicencio
Tunja
Socorro
Bucaramanga
Barrancabermeja
Parque Nacional Paramillo
Cúcuta
San Cristóbal
Sierra Nevada del Cocuy 5493
Yopal
Puerto Carreño
Puerto Ayacucho
Puerto Inírida
Puerto López
Meta
Guaviare
Parque Nacional Tinigua
Parque Nacional Cord. de los Picachos
Garzón
Florencia
Campoalegre
Parque Nacional Cordillera de la Macarena
Parque Nacional Sumapaz
Cerro El 4560
Nevado de Huila
Popayán
Volcán de Puracé 4580
San José del Guaviare
Parque Nacional Sanquianga
Santander
Tumaco

CORDILLERA OCCIDENTAL
CORDILLERA CENTRAL
CORDILLERA ORIENTAL

VENEZUELA
Orinoco
El Tigre
Parque Nacional Cinaruco-Capanaparo
Parque Nacional El Tuparro
Parque Nacional Canaima
La Gran Sabana
Serra Pacaraima
Negro
Casiquiare
Parque Nacional Duida-Marahuaca
Co Yaví 2285
Parque Nacional Jaua Sarisariñama
Parque Nacional Serranía de la Neblina
Parque Nacional Parima-Tapirapecó
Cucuí

© Collins

1:14M

KM   MILES
700 400
600
500 300
400 200
300
200 100
100
0   0

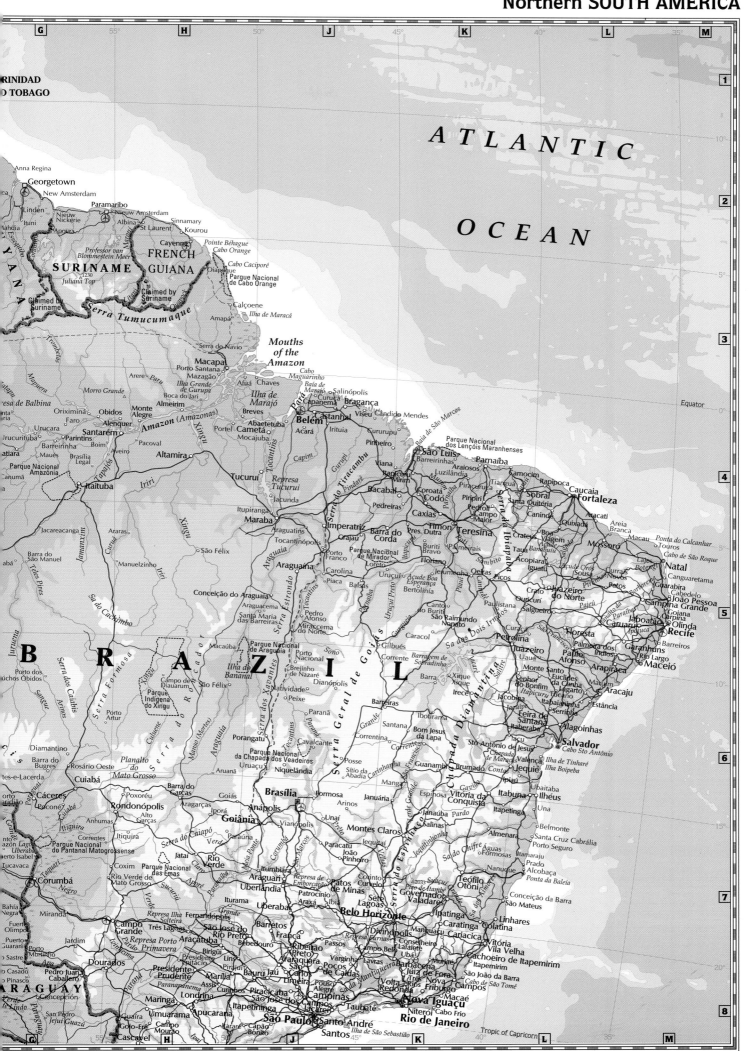

ATLANTIC

OCEAN

TRINIDAD
AND TOBAGO

Anna Regina
Georgetown
New Amsterdam
Linden
Paramaribo
Ituni
Nieuw Nickerie
Albina
Nieuw Amsterdam
St Laurent
Kourou
Cayenne
Pointe Béhague
Cabo Orange
Professor van
Blommestein Meer
FRENCH
GUIANA
Diapoque
Cabo Caciporé
SURINAME
Juliana Top
Claimed by
Suriname
Parque Nacional
de Cabo Orange
Claimed by
Suriname
Serra Tumucumaque
Calçoene
Amapá
Ilha de Maracá
Serra do Navio
Mouths
of the
Amazon
Equator

Macapá
Porto Santana
Mazagão
Ilha Grande
de Gurupá
Afuá
Chaves
Cabo
Maguarinho
Baía de
Marajó
Salinópolis
Morro Grande
Almeirim
Breves
Capanema
Bragança
Viseu
Candido Mendes
Obidos
Monte
Alegre
Ilha de
Marajó
Abaetetuba
Belém
Castanhal
Acará
Cametá
Irituia
Pinheiro
Cururupu
Viana
São Luís
Santarém
Alenquer
Portel
Mocajuba
Capim
Barreirinhas
Parque Nacional
dos Lençóis Maranhenses
Parintins
Boim
Pacoval
Brasília
Legal
Altamira
Tucuruí
Represa
Tucuruí
Jacundá
Bacabal
Coroatá
Piripiri
Itapecuru
Mirim
Piracuruca
Tianguá
Itapipoca
Caucaia
Fortaleza
Itaituba
Iriri
Itupiranga
Imperatriz
Caxias
Codó
Campo
Maior
Santa Quitéria
Canindé
Quixadá
Aracati
Marabá
Araguatins
Barra do
Corda
Timon
Teresina
Crateús
Tauá
Acopiara
Iguatu
Mossoró
Macau
Ponta do Calcanhar
Tocantinópolis
Crajaú
Porto
Franco
Parque Nacional
de Mirador
Loreto
Floriano
Palmeiras
Picos
Oeiras
Jerumenha
Sousa
Currais
Novos
Natal
Conceição do Araguaia
Carolina
Piaca
Balsas
Uruçuí
Açude Boa
Esperança
Bertolínia
Paulistana
Ouricuri
Crato
Juazeiro
do Norte
Patos
Guarabira
João Pessoa
Campina
Grande
Santa Maria
das Barreiras
Pedro
Afonso
Miracema
do Norte
São
Raimundo
Nonato
Canto
do Buriti
Salgueiro
Goiana
Olinda
Recife
Macaúba
Parque Nacional
de Araguaia
Porto
Nacional
Caracol
Sa dos Dois Irmãos
Petrolina
Juazeiro
Floresta
Palmares
Caruaru
Jaboatão
Ilha do
Bananal
Brejinho
de Nazaré
Dianópolis
Gilbués
Corrente
Barragem de
Sobradinho
Barra
Uauá
Paulo
Afonso
Arapiraca
Maceió
Peixe
Natividade
Parana
Barreiras
Xique
Xique
Senhor
do Bonfim
Euclides
da Cunha
Marituba
Porangatu
Cavalcante
Correntina
Santana
Bom Jesus
da Lapa
Irecê
Jacobina
Tucano
Serrinha
Aracaju
Estância
Parque Nacional
da Chapada dos Veadeiros
Posse
Sítio da
Abadia
Uruaçu
Niquelândia
Sto Antônio de Jesus
Santo
Antônio de Jesus
Valença
Feira de
Santana
Itaberaba
Alagoinhas
Salvador
Cabo Sto Antônio
Guanambi
Ipiaú
Jequié
Ilha de Tinharé
Ilha Boipeba
Brumado
Contas
Cuiabá
Barra do
Garças
Goiás
Aragarças
Brasília
Formosa
Januária
Espinosa
Vitória da
Conquista
Itabuna
Ilhéus
Rondonópolis
Iporá
Anápolis
Unaí
Montes Claros
Itapetinga
Una
Goiânia
Vianópolis
Arinos
Janaúba
Salinas
Itamaraju
Belmonte
Jataí
Paraúna
Corumbá
Paracatu
João
Pinheiro
Pardo
Santa Cruz Cabrália
Porto Seguro
Rio
Verde
Itumbiara
Patos
de Minas
Curvelo
Teófilo
Otoni
Prado
Alcobaça
Ponta da Baleia
Araguari
Uberlândia
Patrocínio
Corinto
Sete
Lagoas
Governador
Valadares
Conceição da Barra
São Mateus
Uberaba
Araxá
Ibiá
Belo Horizonte
Ipatinga
Caratinga
Linhares
Colatina
Campo
Grande
Três Lagoas
São José do
Rio Preto
Franca
Divinópolis
Manhuaçu
Cariacica
Vitória
Vila Velha
Cachoeiro de Itapemirim
Itapemirim
São João da Barra
Campos
Macaé
Rio de Janeiro
Cabo Frio
Ilha de São Sebastião
São Paulo
Santo André
Santos
Niterói
Nova Iguaçu

B R A Z I L

P A R A G U A Y

Tropic of Capricorn

1:15M

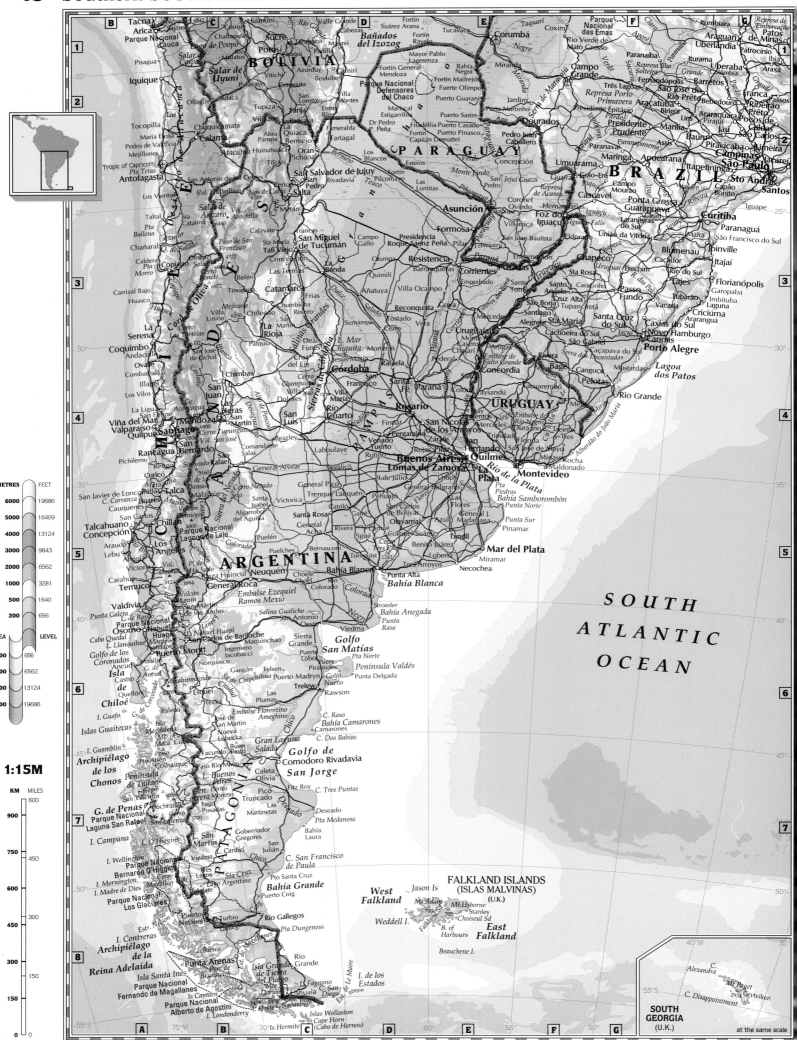

1:15M

Lambert Azimuthal Equal Area Projection

© Collins

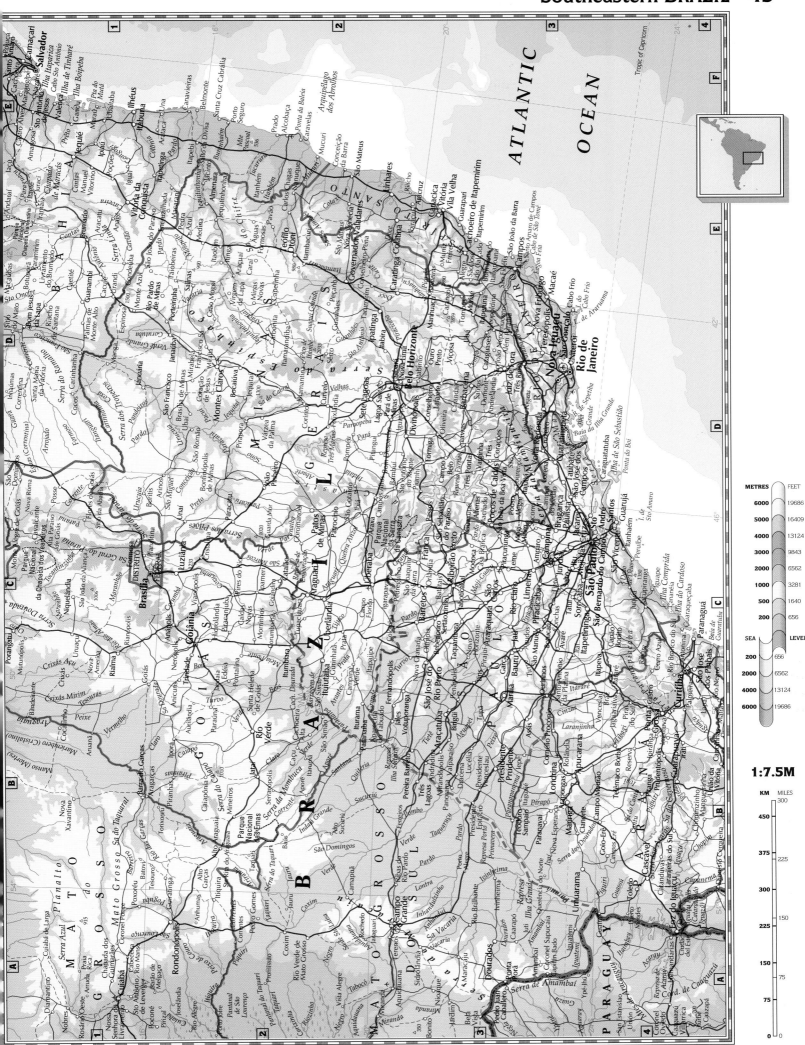

ATLANTIC

OCEAN

METRES / FEET
6000 / 19686
5000 / 16409
4000 / 13124
3000 / 9843
2000 / 6562
1000 / 3281
500 / 1640
200 / 656
SEA LEVEL
200 / 656
2000 / 6562
4000 / 13124
6000 / 19686

1:7.5M

KM MILES
300
450 / 225
375 / 150
300 / 75
225
150
75
0 / 0

Lambert Azimuthal Equal Area Projection

© Collins

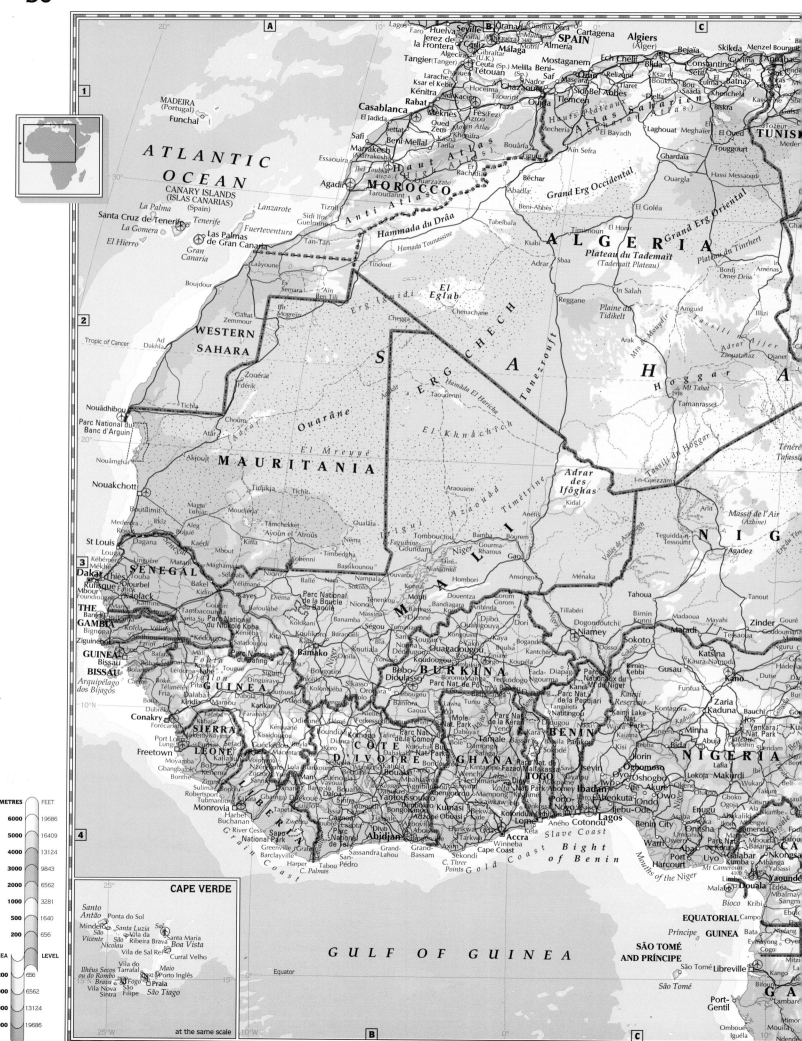

Lambert Azimuthal Equal Area Projection

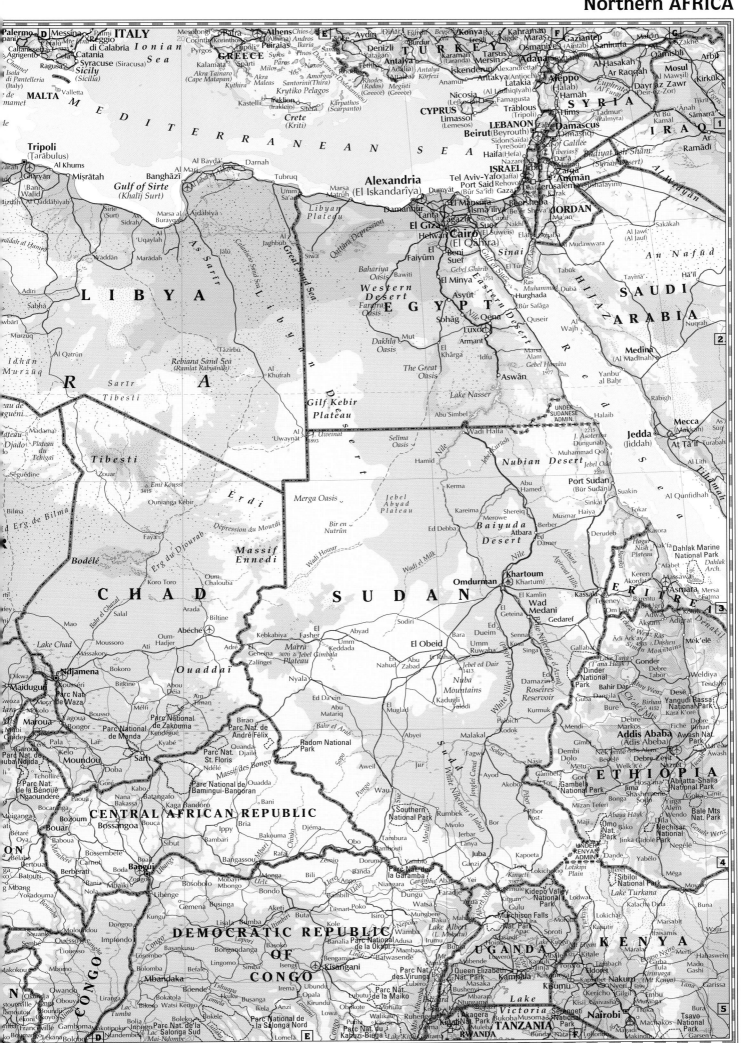

© Collins

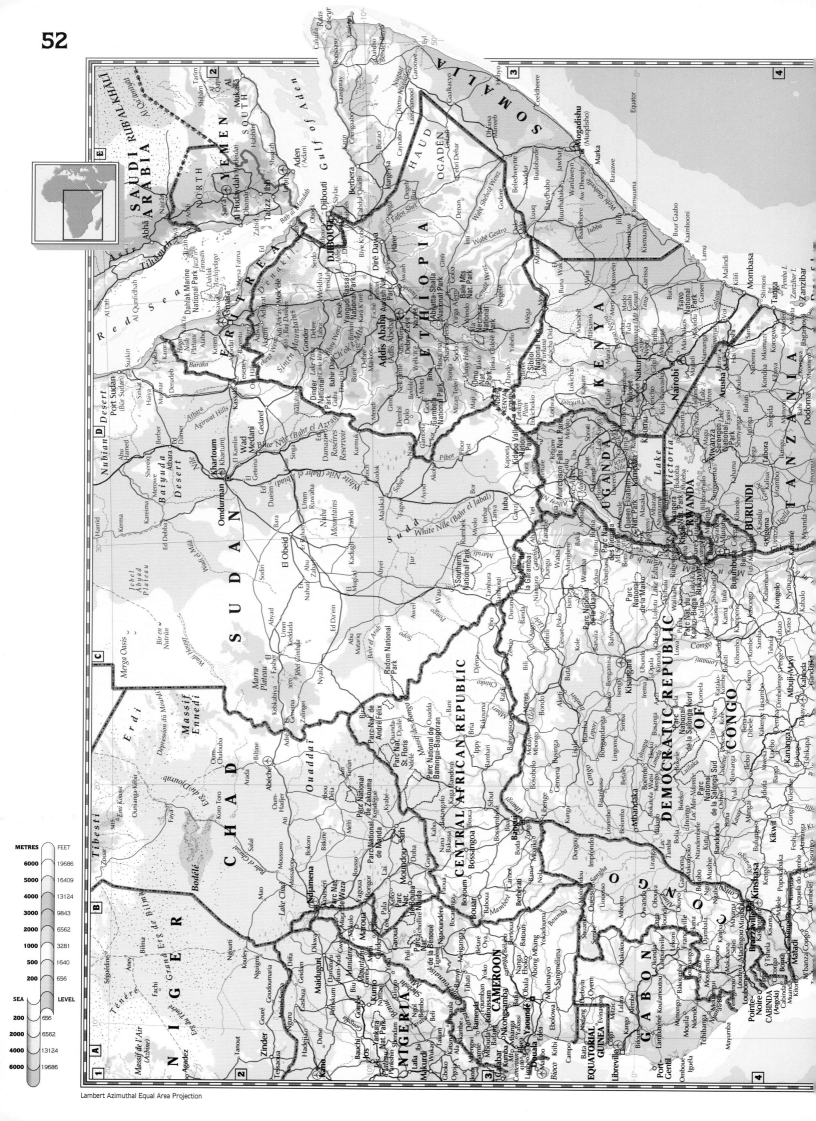

Lambert Azimuthal Equal Area Projection

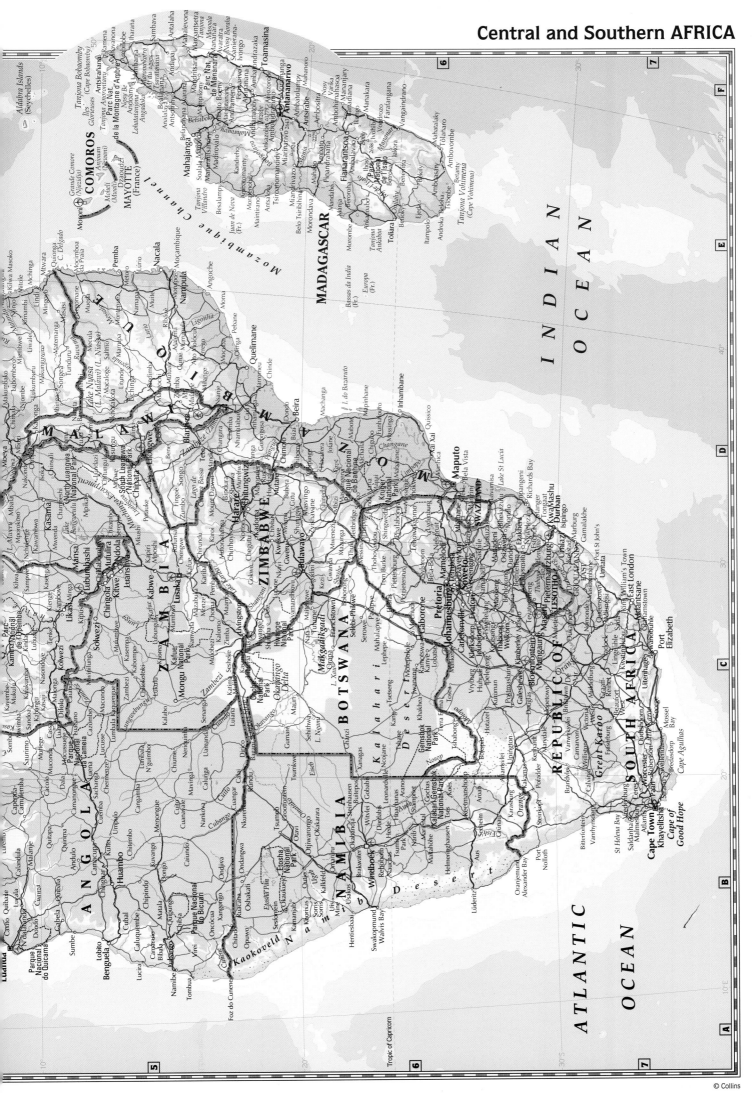

ATLANTIC OCEAN

INDIAN OCEAN

Mozambique Channel

COMOROS

MAYOTTE (France)

MADAGASCAR

MOZAMBIQUE

MALAWI

ZAMBIA

ANGOLA

ZIMBABWE

BOTSWANA

NAMIBIA

Namib Desert

Kalahari Desert

REPUBLIC OF SOUTH AFRICA

LESOTHO

SWAZILAND

Aldabra Islands (Seychelles)

Tropic of Capricorn

Cape of Good Hope

Cape Agulhas

1:16M

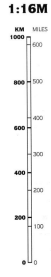

KM MILES
1000 — 600
800 — 500
— 400
600 — 300
400 — 200
200 — 100
0 — 0

© Collins

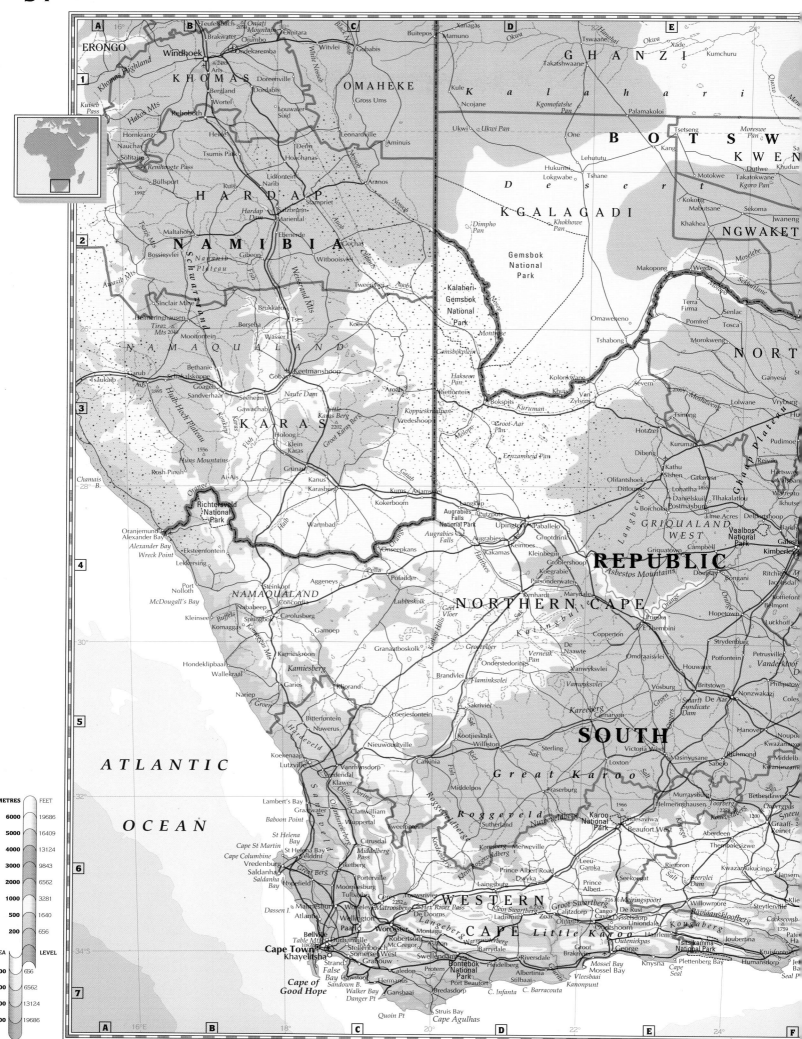

Lambert Azimuthal Equal Area Projection

1:5M

KM MILES

INDEX

THE INDEX includes most of the names on the maps in the atlas. The names are generally indexed to the largest scale map on which they appear. For large physical features this will be the largest scale map on which they appear in their entirety or in the majority. Names can be located using the grid reference letter and numbers around the map frame. Names on insets have a symbol: □ .

Abbreviations used to describe features in the index are explained on the right.

b.	bay	hd	headland	plat., Plat.	plateau
c.	cape	i., I.	island	pt, Pt	point
chan., Chan.	channel	in.	inlet	r.	river
des.	desert	is, Is	islands	reg.	region
div.	division	isth.	isthmus	Rep.	Republic
est.	estuary	l., L.	lake	rf	reef
for.	forest	lag.	lagoon	str., Str.	strait
g., G.	gulf	mt, Mt	mountain	terr.	territory
gl.	glacier	mts, Mts	mountains	v.	valley
h.	hill, hills	pen., Pen.	peninsula	volc.	volcano

A

16C5 Aachen
16E6 Aalen
16B5 Aalst
50C4 Aba
26C3 Ābādān
26D3 Abadeh
50B1 Abadla
49D2 Abaeté r.
47J4 Abaetetuba
50C4 Abakaliki
24L4 Abakan
28A1 Abakanskiy Khrebet mts
46D6 Abancay
25D3 Abarqū
30K1 Abashiri
30K2 Abashiri-gawa r.
30K1 Abashiri-wan b.
24L4 Abaya
41H6 Abbeville
18E1 Abbeville
51E3 Abéché
50B4 Abengourou
11L9 Abenrá
50C4 Abeokuta
36G2 Abercrombie r.
13D6 Aberdare
42C3 Aberdeen
14F3 Aberdeen
40G2 Aberdeen
40B2 Aberdeen
13D6 Abergavenny
13C5 Aberystwyth
26C5 Abhā
50B4 Abidjan
31H6 Abiko
40G5 Abilene
13F6 Abingdon
23F6 Abinsk
39K5 Abitibi, Lake l.
50B4 Aboisso
50C4 Abomey
51D4 Abong Mbang
49E2 Abrolhos, Arquipélago dos
40D3 Absaroka Range mts
26D4 Abu Dhabi
50C4 Abuja
31H5 Abukuma-gawa r.
31H5 Abukuma-kochi plat.
46E6 Abunã r.
27F4 Abu Road
44D4 Acambaro
44C5 Acaponeta
44E5 Acapulco
47J4 Acará
47K4 Acaraú r.
49A4 Acaray r.
46E2 Acarigua
44F5 Acayucán
44F5 Accra
12E4 Accrington
15A4 Achill Island i.
24L4 Achinsk
14C3 A'Chraliag mt
20F6 Acireale
45K4 Acklins Island i.
47L5 Acopiara
19B1 A Coruña
20C2 Acqui Terme
20G5 Acri
41G5 Ada
19D2 Adaja r.
42E1 Adams
43B2 Adams Peak mt
27G6 Adam's Peak mt
26B3 Adana
50A2 Ad Dakhla
26D4 Ad Dammām
52D3 Addis Ababa
26C3 Ad Dīwānīyah
13G6 Addlestone
26C5 Aden
52E2 Aden, Gulf of g.
52D2 Adīgrat
51D2 Adīrī
41M3 Adirondack Mts
52D2 Adīs 'Alem
17N7 Adjud
34F1 Admiralty Gulf b.
34J2 Admiralty Islands
18D5 Adour r.
20F6 Adrano
50B2 Adrar
50C3 Adrar des Ifôghas reg.
41K3 Adrian
20E2 Adriatic Sea
52D2 Ādwa
25P3 Adycha r.
23F6 Adygeya, Respublika div.
50B4 Aézopé
21L5 Aegean Sea
19B1 A Estrada
26E3 Afghanistan
47H4 Afuá
26B3 Afyon
50C3 Agadez
50C2 Agadir
24J5 Agadyr'
29G5 Agana
21M6 Agathonisi i.
18E4 Agde
31G5 Agen
23F5 Aghkev's
19E2 Alcobaça
27G2 Agra
18D2 Agri
20E6 Agrigento
13G6 Aldershot
13F5 Aldridge
20F4 Agropoli
45L5 Aguadilla
45H7 Aguadulce
49B2 Aguapei r.
49A3 Aguaray Guazú r.
49E2 Águas Formosas
19F4 Águilas
54C3 Agulhas, Cape c.

49D3 Agulhas Negras mt
37F3 Ahimanawa Ra.
11U7 Ahtme
37B6 Ahuriri r.
26C3 Ahvāz
31F6 Aichi
21K6 Aigina i.
21K4 Aigio
14C5 Ailsa Craig i.
49E2 Aimorés, Sa dos h.
50C1 Aïn Beïda
19H4 Aïn Defla
19H5 Aïn el Hadjel
50B1 Aïn Sefra
19H4 Aïn Taya
19G5 Aïn Tédélès
19D4 Air Force l. i.
50C3 Aïr, Massif de l' mts
18G2 Aisne r.
19F3 Aitana mt
17L7 Aiud
18G5 Aix-en-Provence
18G4 Aix-les-Bains
27H4 Aizawl
11T8 Aizkraukle
31G5 Aizu-wakamatsu
20C4 Ajaccio
37D5 Ajax, Mt mt
30J2 Ajdabiya
26D4 Ajmer
21K4 Akhisar
23H5 Akhtubinsk
30D7 Aki
31H4 Akita
31H4 Akita
24G5 Akjoujt
10P3 Akkajaure l.
30E6 Akō
26C3 Al Kūt
16B4 Alkmaar
16B4 Alkmaar
27G4 Allahabad
41K3 Akron
27F3 Aksai Chin terr.
23F6 Aksay
27G2 Aksu
52D2 Aksum
24G5 Aktau
24G4 Aktyubinsk
30C7 Akune
10D4 Akureyri
19F3 Almansa
19D2 Almanzor mt
51E1 Al Marj
49C1 Almas, Rio das r.
24J5 Almaty
47H4 Almeirim
16C4 Almelo
49E2 Almenara
19C3 Almendralejo
19E4 Almería
19E4 Almería, Golfo de g.
24G4 Al'met'yevsk
26C4 Al Mubarraz
26C5 Al Mukallā
21L7 Almyrou, Ormos b.
53E5 Andilamena
53E5 Andilanatoby
53H7 Andiyskoye Koysu r.
26F2 Andizhan
47J5 Andoany
19G1 Andoain
19G1 Andorra
19G1 Andorra la Vella
43J5 Andover
10O2 Andøya i.
49B3 Andradina
49D3 Andrelândia
20G4 Andria
21L6 Andros i.
21L7 Andros i.
23D5 Andrushivka
19D3 Andújar
53B5 Anegada
45M5 Anegada, Bahía b.
50C4 Aného
48C6 Anegada, Bahía b.
16E6 Aneto mt
25M4 Angara r.
28C1 Angarsk
44B3 Angel de la Guarda i.
30C7 Arbil
18D3 Arcachon
47L5 Arapiraca
49B3 Araponga
49B2 Araranguá
49B4 Araras, Serra das mts
26C3 Ararat, Mount mt
26B3 Ararat Lerr mt
31G5 Ara-gawa r.
19F1 Aragón r.
19F1 Aragón r.
47J5 Araguaia r.
49C2 Araguari
49C2 Araguari r.
23H7 Aragvi r.
31G5 Arai
47K4 Araiosos
26C3 Arāk
39N4 Arakan Yoma mts
26D3 Aras r.
26D3 Aras r.
19D2 Aranda de Duero
21J2 Aranđelovac
15C3 Aran Island i.
15B4 Aran Islands is
19E2 Aranjuez
42A2 Ashtabula
12E4 Ashton-under-Lyne

B

49A4 Babaeski
46C4 Babahoyo
52E2 Bab al Mandab str.
38F4 Babine
38F4 Babine r.
29D6 Babuyan Islands
47K4 Bacabal
29E5 Bacan i.
17M4 Bacău
15C6 Beacon mt
52B4 Bambari
52B4 Bambari
31F6 Bamberg
26E3 Bamiyan
51D4 Bamenda
47H6 Bananal, Ilha do i.
13F5 Banbridge
13F6 Banbury
45M5 Basse Terre
26D3 Bafq
26B2 Bafra
26D4 Bāft
52D4 Bafoussam
52B4 Bafoulabé
52D4 Bafatá
20D2 Badia Polesine
16F7 Bad Ischl
16E5 Bad Kissingen
16C6 Bad Kreuznach
16D6 Bad Mergentheim
20F3 Atessa
38B4 Athabasca, Lake l.
16E4 Bad Schwartau
35J1 Badu l. i.
26D3 Badulla
50D4 Bafang
29C6 Ban Hat Yai
51D1 Banī Walīd
20G2 Banja Luka
29D7 Banjarmasin
50A3 Banjul
11T8 Bauska
16G5 Bautzen
54E6 Baviaanskloofberg
40E2 Bavispe r.
29D7 Bawean i.
50B3 Bawku
28C2 Bayanhongor
50C4 Benue r.

50C1 Batna
41H5 Baton Rouge
51D4 Batouri
27G6 Bangladesh
27G4 Bangladesh
20F4 Battipaglia
20F4 Battipaglia
41J3 Battle Creek
29B7 Batu, Pulau Pulau is
29F7 Baubau
50C3 Bauchi
20G2 Baja Luka
11T8 Bauska
16G5 Bautzen
54E6 Baviaanskloofberg
40E2 Bavispe r.
29D7 Bawean i.
50B3 Bawku
28C2 Bayanhongor
24G4 Baymak
46E6 Bayano, Laguna lag.
18D5 Bayonne
16E6 Bayreuth
42E2 Bay Shore
13H7 Beachy Head hd
42E2 Beacon
55G6 Beacon Bay
13G6 Beaconsfield
34F1 Beagle Gulf b.
48C8 Beagle, Canal chan.

50C4 Benin City
50B1 Beni-Saf
51F2 Beni Suef
48E5 Benito Juárez
46E4 Benjamin Constant
14D2 Ben Klibreck mt
14D4 Ben Lawers mt
14D4 Ben Lomond mt
14D4 Ben Macdui mt
14E3 Ben More mt
14D4 Ben More mt
14G5 Ben More mt
54E6 Ben More Assynt mt
14C4 Ben Nevis mt
55H3 Benoni
35H2 Bentinck I. i.
12F4 Bentley
12F4 Benue r.
50C4 Benue r.
14D3 Ben Vorlich mt
14D3 Ben Wyvis mt
28E2 Benxi
50B4 Béoumi
30C7 Beppu
21H4 Berat
29F7 Berau, Teluk b.
52E2 Berbera
52B3 Berbérati
28A1 Berdsk
23F6 Berdyans'k
23D5 Berdychiv
23B5 Berehove
21M5 Bergama
20C2 Bergamo
16E5 Bergheim
16C5 Bergisch
18E4 Bergerac
16C5 Bergisch Gladbach
54E4 Berhove
38B3 Bering Sea
25T4 Bering Sea
38B3 Bering Strait str.
43A3 Berkeley
16F4 Berlin
41N3 Bermejo r.
48D2 Bermejo r.
45M2 Bermuda terr.
46C7 Berner Alpen mts
14A3 Berneray i.
34C3 Berneray i.
16G2 Bernina Pass pass
16G6 Beroun
16F5 Berounka r.
19H4 Berrouaghia
41L6 Berry Islands is
23D5 Bershad'
47K5 Bertolínia
51D4 Bertoua
46F4 Beruri
41K4 Beckley
42C2 Berwick
12E2 Berwick-upon-Tweed
13D5 Berwyn h.
18H3 Besançon
41J5 Bessemer
42B2 Bethel Park
55H4 Bethlehem
55H4 Bethlehem
16C7 Bern
24J5 Betpak-Dala plain
26B3 Beira
26D3 Béja
13H6 Bexhill
21H7 Beyşehir Gölü l.
18F5 Béziers
28B4 Bhawm
27G4 Bhilwara
27H4 Bhima r.
27F4 Bhopal
27G4 Bhubaneshwar
27H4 Bhutan
27G4 Biała Podlaska
16G4 Białogard
17L4 Białystok
16H4 Białystok
18D5 Biarritz
30D2 Bibai
16D6 Biberach an der Riß
13F6 Bicester
21D6 Bichvint'a
35H1 Bickerton I. i.
13D6 Bideford
13D6 Bideford Bay b.
17L4 Biebrza r.
16C7 Biel/Bienne
21D2 Biên Hoa
23D5 Bielawa
20C2 Biella
17L4 Bielsk Podlaski
21D2 Biga Yarımadası
23F6 Biga Yarımadası
21J6 Biggleswade
20E2 Bighorn r.
40E2 Bighorn Mountains mts
42B4 Big Otter r.
43D3 Big Smokey Valley
40F5 Big Spring
27G4 Bihar div.
17L7 Bihor, Vârful mt
50A3 Bijagós
23F6 Bijelina
23D6 Bileca
21J3 Bilecik
23E6 Bilhorod-Dnistrovs'kyy
13H6 Billericay

Billingham
Billings
Bill of Portland hd
Biloxi
Bilpa Morea Claypan
Biltine
Bilyayivka
Bimberi, Mt mt
Binaia, G. mt
Bindura
Bingen am Rhein
Bingerville
Binghamton
Bintulu
Bintuhan
Bío Bío r.
Bío r.
Bioco i.
Biokovo mts
Birao
Birecik
Birhan mt
Birigüi
Birjand
Birkenhead
Birkirkara
Birmingham
Birmingham
Birnin-Kebbi
Birnin Konni
Birobidzhan
Birstall
Birżai
Biscay, Bay of
Bischofshofen
Bishkek
Bisho
Bishop Auckland
Bishop's Stortford
Biskra
Bismarck
Bismarck Archipelago i.
Bismarck Range mts
Bismarck Sea
Bissa, Djebel mt
Bissau
Bistriţa r.
Bistriţa r.
Bitola
Bitonto
Bitterroot Range mts
Bityug r.
Biu
Biysk
Bizen
Bizerte
Bjelovar
Bla Bheinn mt
Blackburn
Black Butte
Black Butte L. l.
Black Hills h.
Black Isle i.
Black Mountain
Black Mt mt
Black Mts h.
Black Nossob r.
Blackpool
Blacksburg
Black Sea
Blackstairs Mts
Black Sugarloaf mt
Black Volta r.
Blackwater r.
Blackwater r.
Blackwater r.
Blackwater r.
Blackwater r.
Blagoevgrad
Blagoveshchensk
Blanca, Bahía b.
Blanc, Mont mt
Blanco r.
Blanco r.
Blanda r.
Blandford
Blankenberge
Blantyre
Blessington Lakes
Bletchley
Blida
Block l.
Block Island Sound chan.
Bloemfontein
Bloemhof Dam
Bloomington
Bloomington
Blosseville Kyst
Bluefield
Bluefields
Blue Mountain Pass
Blue Mountains
Blue Mountains
Blue Nile r.
Blue Ridge mts
Blue Stack mt
Blue Stack Mts h.
Blumenau
Blyth
Blythe
Blytheville
Bo
Boac
Boardman
Boa Viagem
Boa Vista r.
Boa Vista i.
Boa Boamby, Tanjona c.
Bobo-Dioulasso
Bobrov
Bobrovytsya
Boby mt
Boca do Acre
Bocas del Toro
Bochnia
Bochum
Bodaybo
Bodélé reg.
Boden
Bodmin
Bodmin Moor reg.
Bodø
Boende
Boggabri
Boggeragh Mts h.
Bognor Regis
Bog of Allen reg.
Bogong, Mt mt
Bogor
Bogorodsk
Bogotá
Boguchany

28D3 Bo Hai g.
55H4 Bohlokong
16F6 Böhmer Wald
16F6 Böhmer Wald mts
29E6 Bohol Sea
27G2 Bohu
23D5 Bohuslav
49C1 Bois r.
40C3 Boise
26D3 Bojnūrd
22E3 Boksitogorsk
50A3 Bolama
27G2 Bole
50B3 Bolgatanga
23D6 Bolhrad
46F7 Bolivia
23H7 Bolnisi
52B4 Bolobo
20D2 Bologna
22E3 Bologoye
24K4 Bolotnoye
10X3 Bol'shaya Imandra, Oz. l.
25M2 Bol'shevik, O. i.
25S3 Bol'shoy Aluy r.
23J5 Bol'shoy Uzen' r.
44D3 Bolson de Mapimí des.
12E4 Bolton
26B2 Bolu
20D1 Bolzano
36H3 Bomaderry
49D1 Bom Despacho
49D1 Bom Jesus da Lapa
14E3 Bom Jesus do Itabapoana
50□ Brava i.
40C5 Bonaire i.
15E4 Bonar Bridge
47H6 Bonaparte Archipelago i.
52C3 Bondo
50B4 Bondoukou
29E7 Bonerate, Kepulauan is
14E4 Bo'ness
48C3 Bonete, Cerro mt
29E7 Bone, Teluk b.
49D2 Bonfinópolis de Minas
52C3 Bongandanga
33E5 Bongolava mts
51D3 Bongor
50B4 Bongouanou
20C4 Bonifacio, Strait of
20D1 Bonin
49A3 Bonito
16C5 Bonn
36C4 Bonney, L. l.
14E5 Bonnyrigg
29E5 Bontoc
29D7 Bontosunggu
36D2 Boolaboolka L. l.
15D5 Booley Hills h.
52E2 Boosaaso
39J2 Boothia, Gulf of
39J2 Boothia Peninsula
13E4 Bootle
51F1 Bor
21K2 Bor
11N8 Borås
45N6 Bordertown
13E5 Bridgnorth
47H4 Borba
47L5 Borborema, Planalto da plat.
18D4 Bordeaux
38G2 Borden I. i.
19J4 Bordj Bou Arréridj
14A3 Boreray i.
10C4 Borgarnes
20B2 Borgo San Dalmazzo
20D3 Borgo San Lorenzo
22G3 Borgosesia
23G5 Borisoglebsk
23G7 Borivli
11O6 Borlänge
29D6 Borneo i.
11O9 Bornholm i.
21M5 Bornova
24K3 Borodino
22E3 Borovichi
17M7 Borşa
25M5 Borshchovochnyy Khrebet mts
26C3 Borūjerd
23B5 Boryslav
23D5 Boryspil'
25N4 Borzya
20G2 Bosanska Dubica
20G2 Bosanska Gradiška
20G2 Bosanska Krupa
20G2 Bosanski Novi
20G2 Bosanski Grahovo
28C4 Bose
20G2 Bosnia-Herzegovina
52B3 Bosobolo
21N4 Bosporus str.
52B3 Bossangoa
52B3 Bossembélé
13G5 Boston
42F1 Boston
41H4 Boston Mts mts
36H2 Botany Bay b.
21L3 Botev mt
21K3 Botevgrad
20G4 Bothnia, Gulf of
23H5 Botkul', Ozero l.
17P5 Botoşani
55G4 Botshabelo
53C6 Botswana
20G5 Botte Donato, Monte mt
49D1 Botucatu
50B4 Bouaflé
50B4 Bouaké
52B3 Bouar
50B1 Bou Arfa
29D6 Bougainville I.
16B5 Bougouni
10H4 Boujdour
40E3 Boulder City
18F2 Boulogne-Billancourt
16H5 Boulogne-sur-Mer
50B3 Boulsa
52B4 Boumba r.
10H4 Boumerdès
50B4 Boundi
43C3 Boundary Peak
18G3 Bourg-en-Bresse
18J3 Bourges
18G3 Bourgogne reg.
13F7 Bournemouth
50C4 Bouna
20C6 Bou Salem
50A3 Boutilimit
38G4 Bове, Mt mt
41J4 Bowling Green
23E7 Boyabat

15E4 Boyne r.
23H7 Büyük Hinaldağ mt
46C3 Buga
20G2 Bugojno
17N7 Buhusi
52C4 Bujumbura
52C4 Bukavu
26E3 Bukhara
18E1 Bülach
48C2 Calama
29D5 Calamian Group
21M5 Bukittinggi
27G5 Brahmapur
28B4 Brahmaputra r.
21M2 Brăila
47J4 Bragança
24G4 Buaya
36F4 Buller, Mt mt
36D4 Buloke, Lake l.
52B4 Bulungu
52C3 Bumba
21M2 Bráila
34D5 Bunbury
35L3 Bundaberg
30D7 Bungo-suidō chan.
30C7 Bungo-takada
52D3 Bunia
29C5 Buôn Mê Thuột
49E2 Buranhaém r.
52E4 Burao
54C4 Buraydah
43C4 Burbank
45J4 Burdekin r.
26B3 Burdur
52D2 Bure
13J5 Bure r.
25M4 Bureinskiy Khrebet mts
21M3 Burgas
13G7 Burgess Hill
19E1 Burgos
21M5 Burhaniye
47K5 Buriti Bravo
49C1 Buritis
50B3 Burkina
43D2 Burlington
41H3 Burlington
16F6 Burley
35K7 Burleigh
12E4 Burnley
14F2 Burray i.
21J4 Burrel
19F3 Burriana
44D3 Burro, Serranías del mts
34D6 Burrow Head hd
26A2 Bursa
13F5 Burton upon Trent
29E7 Buru i.
52D4 Burundi
50C4 Buron
23B4 Bury
13H5 Bury St Edmunds
15E2 Bush r.
29E7 Büsheir
52D4 Bushenyi
52C3 Businga
20C2 Busto Arsizio
52C3 Buta
52C4 Butare
14C5 Bute i.
14C5 Bute, Sound of chan.
55H4 Butha Buthe
42B2 Butler
29E7 Buton i.
40D2 Butte
29C6 Butterworth
14B2 Butt of Lewis hd
39J4 Button Bay b.
29E6 Butuan
32E5 Buturlinovka
22G5 Buurhabaka
13F4 Buxton
22G3 Buy
21M6 Büyükmenderes r.
21M2 Buzău
30C7 Buzen
24G4 Buzuluk
23G5 Buzuluk
42F2 Buzzards Bay b.
35L1 Bwagaoia
22D4 Byarezina r.
44B2 Byaroza
46C4 Cañar
16J4 Bydgoszcz
22D4 Bykhaw
39L2 Bylot Island i.
25M2 Byrranga, Gory mts
25P3 Bytantay r.
16J5 Bytom
16J3 Bytów

17K4 Bug r.
46C3 Buga
20G2 Bugojno
17N7 Buhusi
52C4 Bujumbura
52C4 Bukavu
26E3 Bukhara
22J4 Bula r.
29D5 Calamian Group
51E2 Calanscio Sand Sea des.
29E5 Calapan
21M2 Călăraşi
47H3 Calçoene
27G4 Calcutta
19B3 Caldas da Rainha
49C2 Caldas Novas
40C3 Caldwell
55G5 Caledon r.
48C7 Caleta Olivia
12C3 Calf of Man i.
37E5 California div.
42C2 California
44B2 California, Golfo de g.
43D2 Callaghan, Mt mt
46C6 Callao
20F6 Caltanissetta
53B5 Caluquembe
40F4 Calvo, Monte mt
13H5 Cam r.
49E1 Camaçari
53B5 Camaçupa
14E5 Camarguе
28B2 Camarmângola
13C6 Camarthen
13C6 Camarthen Bay b.
43B2 Carmichael
19D4 Cárdenas
13D4 Carnedd Llywelyn mt
34E4 Carnegie, L.
14C3 Carn Eighe mt
14C3 Carn nan Gabhar mt
52B3 Carnot
47J5 Carolina
37A6 Caroline Pk mt
45K6 Carora
17M7 Carpathian Mountains mts
35H1 Carpentaria, Gulf of g.
18C4 Carpentras
20D2 Carpi
26C7 Carpina
43C4 Carpinteria
19F4 Carra, Lough l.
15B6 Carrantuohill mt
20D2 Carrara
14D5 Carrick reg.
15F3 Carrickfergus
15C4 Carrick-on-Shannon
23F7 Çarşamba
40F5 Carson City
43C2 Carson Lake l.
46C2 Cartagena
19F4 Cartagena
20F4 Cartago
46B3 Cartago
49D3 Campo Belo
49A3 Campo Grande
47K4 Campo Maior
49A3 Campo Mourão
49E3 Campos
49C3 Campos Altos
49D3 Campos do Jordão
49D2 Campos Eré reg.
13D5 Cannock Mts i.
21L2 Câmpina
47L4 Campina Grande
49C3 Campinas
49C2 Campina Verde
45J8 Campoalegre
20F4 Campobasso
49D3 Campo Belo
49A3 Campo Grande
47K4 Campo Maior
47L5 Caruaru
47L4 Caruba
49C2 Campinas
46E3 Carvoeiro
14D5 Carrick reg.
49E2 Carangola
21K2 Caransebeş
45H5 Caratasca, Laguna lag.
49D2 Caratinga
46E4 Carauari
19F3 Caravaca de la Cruz
49E2 Caravelas
42D2 Carbondale
20C5 Carbonia
49D2 Carbonita
19D2 Carcaixent
47H3 Carcassonne
44E4 Cárdenas
48B7 Cardiel, L. l.
13D6 Cardiff
29C2 Cardigan Bay b.
49C4 Cardoso, Ilha do i.
38G4 Cariboo Mountains mts
49D1 Carinhanha
49D1 Carinhanha r.
46F1 Caripito
55G3 Carletonville
12E3 Carlisle
42C2 Carlisle
18E5 Carlit, Pic mt
16G6 České Budějovice
49C4 Carlos Chagas
15E5 Carlow
43D5 Carlsbad
14E5 Carluke
36H2 Carmarthen

51F1 Cairo
20C2 Cairo Montenotte
46C5 Cajamarca
20G1 Čakovec
50C4 Calabar
52C4 Calabar
21K3 Calafat
18E1 Calais
48C2 Calama
29D5 Calamian Group
51E2 Calanscio Sand Sea des.
29E5 Calapan
21M2 Călăraşi
47H3 Calçoene
27G4 Calcutta
19B3 Caldas da Rainha
49C2 Caldas Novas
40C3 Caldwell
55G5 Caledon r.
48C7 Caleta Olivia
12C3 Calf of Man i.
37E5 California div.
42C2 California
44B2 California Aqueduct canal
44B2 California, Golfo de g.
43D2 Callaghan, Mt mt
46C6 Callao
20F6 Caltanissetta
53B5 Caluquembe
40F4 Calvo, Monte mt
13H5 Cam r.
49E1 Camaçari
53B5 Camaçupa
13C6 Camarthen
13C6 Camarthen Bay b.
46C5 Chachapoyas
29C5 Chachoengsao
51D3 Chad
51D3 Chad, Lake l.
26E3 Chaghcharān
13H6 Camberley
29C5 Cambodia
13B7 Camborne
18F1 Cambrai
13D5 Cambrian Mountains reg.
42C3 Cambridge
13H5 Cambridge
42D3 Camden
41H5 Camden
48B8 Camden, Isla i.
43B2 Cameron Park
50D4 Cameroon
52C4 Cameroon, Mt mt
47J4 Cametá
46F6 Camiri
54C4 Camocim
48A7 Campana, I. i.
38F4 Campbell River
44F5 Campeche
44F5 Campeche, Bahía de g.
21L2 Câmpina
47L4 Campina Grande
49C3 Campinas
49C2 Campina Verde
45J8 Campoalegre
20F4 Campobasso
49D3 Campo Belo

49D3 Carandaí
42D2 Carangola
49D2 Carangola
21K2 Caransebeş
45H5 Caratasca, Laguna lag.
49D2 Caratinga
46E4 Carauari
19F3 Caravaca de la Cruz
49E2 Caravelas
42D2 Carbondale
20C5 Carbonia
49D2 Carbonita
19D2 Carcaixent
47H3 Carcassonne
27G4 Cárdenas
44E4 Cárdenas
48B7 Cardiel, L. l.
13D6 Cardiff
29C2 Cardigan Bay b.
49C4 Cardoso, Ilha do i.
17L7 Carei
32E2 Central Ra. mts
38E2 Ceres
54C6 Ceres
20F4 Cerignola
21N2 Cernavodă
21H4 Cérrik
44D4 Cerritos
49C4 Cerro Azul
46C6 Cerro de Pasco
20F4 Cervati, Monte
12E3 Cervia
19D5 Ceuta
18F4 Cévennes mts
46C5 Chachapoyas
29C5 Chachoengsao
51D3 Chad
51D3 Chad, Lake l.
26E3 Chaghcharān
34E4 Chagra r.
14C4 Carn nan Gabhar mt
52B3 Carnot
29E6 Chalatenango
39M5 Chaleur Bay in.
21K5 Chalkida
18C2 Châlons-en-Champagne
18G3 Chalon-sur-Saône
26E3 Chaman
42C3 Chambersburg
18C4 Chambéry
20C7 Chambi, Jebel mt
26E4 Chamba r.
48E4 Chajari
44G6 Chalatenango
39M5 Chaleur Bay in.
21K5 Chalkida
18G3 Chalon-sur-Saône
48D4 Champaqui, Cerro mt
41M3 Champlain, Lake
44F5 Champotón
48B3 Chañaral
38D3 Chandalar r.
27F3 Chandigarh
53B5 Chandler
13J6 Chandrapur
28E2 Changane r.
28D4 Changchun
28D3 Changde
28D4 Changsha
28D3 Changzhou
21H4 Chania
18C2 Channel Islands is
43C5 Channel Islands is
13J6 Channel Tunnel
29C5 Chanthaburi
21L2 Chany, Ozero l.
14D4 Chapada fells h.
22J4 Chapayevsk
48F3 Chapecó
48F3 Chapecó r.
13F4 Chapeltown
26C3 Chardzhev
18E3 Charente r.
24G5 Chari r.
18E4 Charleroi
47J4 Charleston
41L4 Charleston
40C4 Charleston Peak mt
18G2 Charleville-Mézières
31H4 Chōkai-san volc.

38H4 Cedar Lake l.
41H3 Cedar Rapids
44A3 Cedros i.
29E6 Celebes Sea
20F5 Cefalù
17J7 Ceglèd
44D4 Celaya
29E6 Celebes Sea
20F1 Celje
16E4 Celle
42E2 Centereach
55G1 Central div.
52C3 Central African Republic
19D2 Carcaixent
46C5 Central, Cordillera mts
46C5 Central, Cordillera mts
49C4 Central, Cordillera mts
40B2 Centralia
32E2 Central Ra. mts
38E2 Ceres
54C6 Ceres
20F4 Cerignola
21N2 Cernavodă
21H4 Cérrik
44D4 Cerritos
49C4 Cerro Azul
46C6 Cerro de Pasco
20F4 Cervati, Monte
12E3 Cervia
19D5 Ceuta
18F4 Cévennes mts
46C5 Chachapoyas
29C5 Chachoengsao
51D3 Chad
51D3 Chad, Lake l.
26E3 Chaghcharān
34E4 Chagra r.
26E4 Châh Bahār
48E4 Chajari
44G6 Chalatenango
39M5 Chaleur Bay in.
21K5 Chalkida
18C2 Châlons-en-Champagne
18G3 Chalon-sur-Saône
26E3 Chaman
42C3 Chambersburg
18C4 Chambéry
20C7 Chambi, Jebel mt
26E4 Chamba r.
26E4 Chambeshi r.
41J3 Champaign
48D4 Champaqui, Cerro mt
41M3 Champlain, Lake
44F5 Champotón
48B3 Chañaral
38D3 Chandalar r.
27F3 Chandigarh
53B5 Chandler
13J6 Chandrapur
28E2 Changane r.
28D4 Changchun
28D3 Changde
28D4 Changsha
28D3 Changzhou
21H4 Chania
18C2 Channel Islands is
43C5 Channel Islands is
13J6 Channel Tunnel
29C5 Chanthaburi
21L2 Chany, Ozero l.
14D4 Chapada fells h.
22J4 Chapayevsk
48F3 Chapecó
48F3 Chapecó r.
13F4 Chapeltown
26C3 Chardzhev
18E3 Charente r.
24G5 Chari r.
18E4 Charleroi
47J4 Charleston
41L4 Charleston
40C4 Charleston Peak mt
18G2 Charleville-Mézières
31H4 Chōkai-san volc.
52D2 Ch'ok'ē Mts mts
32B3 Chaouèn
28D4 Chaozhou
40B3 Cascade Range mts
21M4 Çan
38G3 Čanada
40F4 Canadian r.
41M4 Çanakkale
42C1 Canandaigua
44B2 Canavea
46C4 Cañar
50A2 Canary Islands is
49C2 Canastra, Serra da mts
41K6 Canaveral, Cape
49A4 Canavieiras
36G3 Canberra
44G4 Cancún
47J4 Cândido Mendes
48E4 Canelones
19C1 Cangas del Narcea
48F4 Canguaretama
38F4 Canguçu r.
39L4 Caniapiscau r.
39L4 Caniapiscau, Lac l.
20E6 Canicattì
47J4 Canindé
42C1 Canindé r.
42C1 Canisteo r.
48E3 Canna r.
14B3 Canna i.
13H5 Cannes
13H5 Cannock
48F3 Canoas
48G4 Canoinhas
19D1 Cantábrica, Cordillera mts
13J6 Canterbury
37C5 Canterbury Bight b.
37C5 Canterbury Plains
29C5 Cần Thơ
47K5 Canto do Buriti
13J6 Canton
49B4 Cantu r.
49B4 Canutama
13H6 Canvey Island
40F4 Canyon
54C6 Cao Bằng
49A4 Capanema r.
49A4 Capão Bonito
38E3 Cape Barren I.
20F5 Capo d'Orlando
20C3 Capraia, Isola di i.
38D4 Capricorn Channel chan.
20F4 Capri, Isola di i.
53B5 Caprivi Strip reg.
46E4 Caquetá r.
42B1 Cayuga
29E5 Cebu
17K3 Cecina
38C2 Cawndilla Lake l.
47K4 Caxias
48F3 Caxias do Sul
53B4 Caxito
20B7 Cayenne
45J5 Cayman Brac i.
45H5 Cayman Islands
42B1 Cayuga
29E5 Cebu
40D1 Cedar City
41H3 Cedar Falls

21L3 Cherven Bryag
23C5 Chervonohrad
13F6 Cherwell r.
41L4 Chesapeake
42C3 Chesapeake Bay
13G6 Chesham
13E4 Cheshire Plain
29C7 Cirebon
13G6 Cheshunt
13E4 Chester
42D3 Chester r.
42D3 Chester r.
13F4 Chesterfield
33F3 Chesterfield, Îles is
42B2 Chestnut Ridge
44G5 Chetumal
13F6 Cheviot Hills h.
40F3 Cheyenne
40F3 Cheyenne r.
19D4 Chiang Mai
29C7 Chiari
31H6 Chiba
31H6 Chiba
41J3 Chicago
13G7 Chichester
34D3 Chichester Range mts
31G6 Chichibu
40F6 Chickamauga r.
40G4 Chickasha
19C4 Chiclana de la Frontera
46C5 Chiclayo
43B2 Chico
48C7 Chico r.
48C7 Chico r.
42E1 Chicopee
39L5 Chicoutimi
16F7 Chiemsee l.
20F3 Chieti
28D2 Chifeng
49E2 Chifre, Serra do mts
44C3 Chihuahua
44C3 Chihuahua div.
40E6 Chikuma-gawa r.
31G5 Chikuma-gawa r.
31G5 Chikushino
21K5 Chalkida
48C3 Chile
48C3 Chilecito
53C5 Chililabombwe
44B5 Chililán
41L4 Chillicothe
40B2 Chilliwack
48B4 Chiloé, Isla de i.
12G4 Cleethorpes
18G4 Chambéry
44E5 Chilpancingo
13E6 Chiltern Hills h.
53C5 Chimanimani
21K5 Chimay
46C5 Chimbote
46C6 Chimboraço, Cerro mt
46C5 Chimbote
52D6 Chimoio
28B3 China
48D4 Chinchaqui, Cerro mt
46C6 Chincha Alta
42D4 Chincoteague B.
53C5 Chingola
27F5 Chip Changsha
21L4 Chinchón
23J4 Chipita
48C6 Chipchihua, Sa de mts
53B5 Chipindo
27F5 Chiplun
13H6 Chippenham
13F6 Chipping Sodbury
13E5 Chipping Norton
13E6 Chipping Campden
44G6 Chiquimula
23G5 Chir r.
31G6 Chino
20E2 Chioggia
21M5 Chios
21L5 Chios i.
53D5 Chipata
48C6 Chipchihua, Sa de mts
53B5 Chipindo
27F5 Chiplun
18C2 Channel Islands is
40E5 Chiricahua
45H7 Chirripó mt
22J4 Chistopol'
25N4 Chita
30J2 Chitose
27F5 Chitradurga
27F5 Chittagong
53C6 Chitungwiza
33F2 Choiseul i.
36G1 Choiseul Sound chan.
18G2 Chojnice
31H4 Chōkai-san volc.
52D2 Ch'ok'ē Mts mts
32B3 Chaouèn
29C5 Chon Buri
29C5 Chʻŏngju
28C3 Chʻŏnan
44G6 Choluteca
16F5 Chomutov
25M3 Chona r.
29C5 Chʻŏnan
29C5 Chon Buri
28C3 Chʻŏngjin
28C3 Chʻŏngju
28C3 Chʻŏnju
28B4 Chongqing
29C5 Chʻŏngju
48F3 Chopim r.
48F3 Chopinzinho
37A7 Chopim r.
12E4 Chorley
16G6 Chortkiv
21L4 Chōshi
23H7 Chechen', Ostrov i.
23H7 Chechenskaya Respublika div.
13F7 Christchurch
37C5 Christchurch
44A2 Christiansø
33G6 Christina, Mt mt
28E3 Christmas Island terr.
30A7 Cheju Do i.
28E3 Cheju-haehyŏp chan.
32F3 Chŭchak
35V3 Chukchi Sea
24K4 Chulym
19E2 Chula Vista
14C3 Chumphon
16G4 Chumphon
29C5 Chumphon
25L4 Chuna r.
28E3 Chŏngju
25M3 Chʻunch'ŏn
29C5 Chʻunch'ŏn
29C5 Chʻʻnju
28C3 Chupara
48B3 Chuquicamata
16D7 Chur
46E1 Churchill
39K4 Churchill
39K4 Churchill r.
46E1 Churuguara
14C3 Chushka
32F3 Chuvashskaya Respublika div.
28D4 Chuxiong
21L2 Ciadar-Lunga
29C7 Cianjur
28C4 Ciechanów
23G6 Cieszyn
19E3 Cieza
21H4 Cigüela r.
28C4 Cijara, Embalse de resr
29C7 Cilacap
43D6 Cima
24G5 Cimişlia

20D2 Cimone, Monte mt
19G2 Cinca r.
41L4 Cincinnati
18J5 Cinto, Monte mt
29C7 Cirebon
20B2 Cirò
20D5 Cirò Marina
13E4 Cirencester
33F3 Cîtlaltépetl, Vol. volc.
20E3 Città di Castello
20E3 Cittanova
21L2 Ciucaş, Vârful mt
44D5 Ciudad Acuña
44D5 Ciudad Altamirano
44F2 Ciudad Bolívar
44C2 Ciudad Camargo
44F5 Ciudad del Carmen
44C3 Ciudad Delicias
44C3 Ciudad de Valles
46F2 Ciudad Guayana
44D5 Ciudad Guzmán
44D5 Ciudad Ixtepec
44C2 Ciudad Juárez
44E4 Ciudad Mante
44C3 Ciudad Obregón
19E3 Ciudad Real
44E4 Ciudad Victoria
21N5 Civan Dağ mt
20E1 Cividale del Friuli
19C4 Civita Castellana
20E3 Civitanova Marche
20D3 Civitavecchia
13J6 Clacton-on-Sea
42C3 Clan Alpine Mts mts
15C4 Clare r.
15A4 Clare Island i.
13E6 Clarence r.
40D2 Clark Fork r.
41H5 Clarksdale
41H4 Clarksville
49B1 Claro r.
49B1 Claro r.
43A3 Clarcond
35L4 Clear, Cape c.
42A1 Clear Creek
41K6 Clearwater
40D2 Clearwater
14C3 Cleethorpes
18F4 Clermont-Ferrand
13E6 Clevedon
41K3 Cleveland
41K4 Cleveland
12F3 Cleveland Hills h.
40D2 Cleveland, Mt mt
42C2 Cleveleys
15B4 Clew Bay b.
15C6 Clear, Cape c.
15B3 Clifden
42B2 Clinton
41H4 Clinton
42G4 Clinton
44C6 Clipperton Island terr.
12E4 Clitheroe
15D5 Clonmel
41K3 Cloud Peak mt
40F5 Clovis
14C3 Cluanie, Loch l.
21N2 Cluj-Napoca
37B6 Clutha r.
13D4 Clwydian Range mts
13D4 Clwyd r.
13D4 Clyde r.
38C3 Clyde Inlet chan.
14D5 Clydebank
14D5 Clyde, Firth of est.
6 Cook Islands terr.
12E4 Clitheroe
49E2 Conselheiro Lafaiete
49E1 Conselheiro Pena
12F3 Coalville
18D7 Constance, Lake l.
40F5 Clovis
14C3 Cluanie, Loch l.
50C1 Constantine
21N2 Cluj-Napoca
49E1 Conselheiro Pena
49E2 Conselheiro Lafaiete
48B4 Aconcagua, Mt mt
40F6 Coahuila div.
12F3 Coalville
23G5 Chir r.
31G6 Coari
46F5 Coari
46F5 Coari r.
12F3 Coatbridge
43C3 Coaldale
14C3 Cluanie, Loch l.
29C5 Chanthaburi
49D3 Coração de Jesus
32F3 Coral Sea
32F3 Coral Sea Islands Territory terr.
49D3 Corangamite, L. l.
13G5 Corby
16H4 Corcoran
46H4 Corcovado, G. de
44G6 Coronado, Baiá de
44B6 Coronados, Golfo de los b.
38G3 Coronation Gulf
40G6 Coronel Oviedo
40G6 Coronel Sapucaia
54F6 Cockscomb mt
44E5 Coco r.
49D1 Corrente
46E1 Corrente r.
48E3 Corrente r.
49B2 Corrente r.
49A2 Corrente r.
48E3 Corrientes
49E2 Corrientes r.
49B4 Corrientes r.
14C3 Corrib, Lough l.
48E3 Corrientes
49E2 Corrientes, Cabo c.
14D6 Corse, Cap hd
18J5 Corsham
13F6 Corsham
18J5 Corsica i.
18J5 Corte
19C4 Cortegana
40E4 Cortez
20D1 Cortina d'Ampezzo
42C2 Cortland
20E3 Corno, Monte mt
23G7 Çoruh r.
26B2 Çorum

42C3 Columbia
49C2 Columbia
41K5 Columbia
41J4 Columbia
41H4 Columbia
40B2 Columbia r.
39L1 Columbia, C. c.
42C3 Columbia, District of div.
38G4 Columbia, Mt mt
40G3 Columbus
41J5 Columbus
41K4 Columbus
41K5 Columbus
43D2 Columbus Salt Marsh
44D5 Colville
37E2 Colville Channel
13D4 Colwyn Bay
20E2 Comacchio
20E2 Comacchio, Valli di lag.
46C4 Comayagua
15D5 Comeragh Mountains h.
44F5 Comitán de Domínguez
42E2 Commack
20C2 Como
20C2 Como, Lago di l.
48C7 Comodoro Rivadavia
53E5 Comoros
18H4 Compiègne
44D4 Compostela
49C4 Comprida, Ilha i.
23D6 Comrat
50A4 Conakry
49A2 Conceição da Barra
49D2 Conceição do Araguaia
48B4 Concepción
48E3 Concepción
44B5 Concepción
48B6 Concepción
44D3 Conchos r.
44D3 Conchos r.
41M3 Concord
43B2 Concord
42E2 Concord
48E4 Concordia
43A3 Concordia
38G5 Concordia
35L4 Condeúba
20E2 Conegliano
42B2 Conemaugh r.
42B2 Coney I. i.
13G6 Congleton
52C4 Congo
52C4 Congo, Dem. Rep.
52B4 Congo r.
41H5 Conn, Lough l.
42G4 Connacht reg.
41M3 Connecticut
42E2 Connecticut div.
48C3 Connellsville
15B4 Connemara reg.
15B3 Conn, Lough l.
41G5 Conroe
49D3 Conselheiro Lafaiete
49E2 Conselheiro Pena
12F3 Consett
18D7 Constance, Lake l.
50C1 Constantine
21N2 Constanţa
29D6 Crocker Range mts
13D4 Conwy
13D4 Conwy r.
6 Cook Islands terr.
38C3 Cook Inlet chan.
37E4 Cook Strait str.
40F6 Coahuila div.
36B3 Coorong, The in.
40B3 Coos Bay
11N9 Copenhagen
48B3 Copiapó r.
20D2 Copparo
38G3 Coppermine
48F3 Copiapó
49D2 Coração de Jesus
33F3 Coral Sea
32F3 Coral Sea Islands Territory terr.
49D3 Corangamite, L. l.
13G5 Corby
16H4 Corcoran
46H4 Corcovado, G. de
44G6 Coronado, Baiá de
14D6 Corrib, Lough l.
40E4 Cortez
40E4 Cortland
20E3 Corno, Monte mt
23G7 Çoruh r.
26B2 Çorum

47G7 Corumbá
49C2 Corumbá r.
40B3 Corvallis
20G5 Cosenza
19F3 Costa Blanca
19H2 Costa Brava
19C4 Costa de la Luz
19D4 Costa del Sol
45H6 Mosquitos, Costa de
45H6 Costa Rica
44C4 Costa Rica
29E6 Cotabato
49E2 Cotaxé r.
18H5 Côte d'Azur
50B4 Côte d'Ivoire
18G2 Côtes de Meuse ridge
13C5 Cothi r.
19G1 Cotiella mt
20E2 Cotonou
46C4 Cotopaxi, Volcán volc.
13E6 Cotswold Hills h.
16G5 Cottbus
41G3 Council Bluffs
11R9 Courland Lagoon
18B5 Couvin
42C3 Cove Mts h.
13F5 Coventry
19C2 Covilhã
36F2 Cowal, L. l.
34E5 Cowan, L. l.
13C6 Cowdenbeath
13F7 Cowes
42B3 Cowpasture r.
49D1 Coxá r.
48E4 Coxilha de Santana h.
49A2 Coxim
27H4 Cox's Bazar
43C3 Coyote Peak mt
21L2 Cozia, Vârful mt
44G4 Cozumel
55F6 Cradock
15E3 Craigavon
36E4 Craigieburn
13F7 Cowes
16E6 Crailsheim
21K2 Craiova
12F2 Cramlington
12F4 Cranbourne
36E5 Cranbourne
38G5 Cranbrook
42F2 Cranston
42F2 Cranston
47K5 Crateús
47L5 Crateús
13G6 Crawley
14D4 Creag Meagaidh mt
20D2 Cremona
20F2 Cres i.
21L7 Crete i.
18E3 Creuse r.
18E3 Crewe
13E4 Crewe
12F2 Cramlington
12F2 Cranbrook
49A3 Criciúma
49C2 Cristalina
46D1 Cristóbal Colón, Pico mt
49C1 Crixás
49C1 Crixás Açu r.
49C1 Crixás Mirim r.
20F2 Croatia
29D6 Crocker Range mts
43B3 Crockett, Mt mt
20G5 Crotone
20G5 Crotone
13H6 Crouch r.
36F1 Crowal r.
13H6 Crowborough
36E2 Crowl r.
13G6 Croydon
13G6 Cruz Alta
48F3 Cruz Alta
48E4 Cruz del Eje
49D3 Cruzeiro
46D5 Cruzeiro do Sul
17K7 Csongrád
53C5 Cuando r.
53B5 Cuango r.
44C3 Cuauhtémoc
45H4 Cuba
53B5 Cubal
53B5 Cubango r.
46C3 Cúcuta
46C4 Cuenca
19E2 Cuenca
19E2 Cuenca, Serranía de mts
44E5 Cuernavaca
43B4 Cuesta Pass pass
46C3 Cugir
49A1 Cuiabá
49A1 Cuiabá r.
14B3 Cuillin Hills mts
14B3 Cuillin Sound chan.
49E2 Cuité r.
53B5 Cuito r.
19C2 Cuito, Serra de la mts
44C4 Culiacán
19E3 Cullera
41J5 Cullman
12F3 Culpepper, Isla i.
47H6 Culuene r.
14D5 Culzean Bay b.
46C3 Cumaná
46C1 Cumaná
46C3 Cumbal, Nevado de mt
49C2 Cumberland
42C3 Cumberland
39M3 Cumberland Peninsula pen.
38C3 Cumberland Peninsula pen.
38G3 Cumberland Plateau plat.
39M3 Cumberland Sound chan.
14E5 Cumbernauld
53B5 Cunene r.
20B2 Cuneo
46C4 Cuorgnè
21J4 Çorovodë
15E6 Curação
44G6 Curaray r.
49A3 Curicó
49C4 Curitiba
49D2 Curnbockbilly, Mt
35L2 Curtis I. i.
47H4 Curuá r.
47K4 Curuçá
47H4 Cururupu
49A2 Cuschaven
44G6 Cusco
44E6 Cusco
20G5 Cuxhaven
13G6 Cwmbran
29E5 Cyangugu
21L6 Cyclades is
38G5 Cypress Hills mts
26B3 Cyprus
16G6 Czech Republic
17J5 Częstochowa

57

D

50B4	Dabakala	52C4	Demba
17J5	Dąbrowa Górnicza	52D3	Dembī Dolo
16E6	Dachau	40E5	Deming
29E5	Daet	21N5	Demirci
50A3	Dagana	29C7	Dempo, G. volc.
23H7	Dagestan, Respublika div.	52E2	Denakil reg.
28D2	Da Hinggan Ling	24H6	Denau
52E2	Dahlak Archipelago is	28C2	Dengkou
20C7	Dahmani	26A3	Denizli
31F6	Dahnichiga-take volc.	16B4	Den Helder
30D6	Daisen volc.	19G3	Denia
50A3	Dakar	26A3	Denizli
51E2	Dakhla Oasis	11M8	Denmark
22D4	Dakol'ka r.	39Q3	Denmark Strait
21J3	Dakovica	14E4	Denny
21H2	Dakovo	29D7	Denpasar
50A3	Dalaba	41G5	Denton
28C2	Dalandzadgad	32F2	D'Entrecasteaux Islands
29C5	Da Lat	34D5	D'Entrecasteaux, Pt pt
42C3	Dalhart	33G3	D'Entrecasteaux, Récifs rf
28C4	Dali	40E4	Denver
28E3	Dalian	27G4	Deogarh
14E5	Dalkeith	23J7	Derbent
41G5	Dalmally	42E2	Derby
20G3	Dalmatia reg.	13F5	Derby
50B4	Dalou	15D3	Derg r.
35K3	Dalrymple, L. l.	23J5	Dergachi
35K3	Dalrymple, Mt mt	15C5	Derg, Lough l.
41K5	Dalton	23F5	Derhachi
15C5	Dalua r.	23F5	Derkul r.
34G1	Daly r.	15D4	Derravaragh, Lough l.
43A3	Daly City	15E5	Derry
27F4	Damanhûr	15C3	Derryveagh Mts
26B3	Damascus	46E7	Desaguadero r.
48B4	Damas, P. de las pass	48C4	Desaguadero r.
50D3	Damaturu	43D2	Desatoya Mts mts
50B4	Damongo	52D2	Desē
34E2	Dampier Land	34E2	Deseado
29F7	Dampir, Selat chan.	41H3	Des Moines
22E4	Danané	41H3	Des Moines r.
29C5	Da Năng	22E4	Desna r.
42E2	Danbury	22E4	Desnogorsk
28E2	Dandong	16F5	Dessau
13E4	Dane r.	16D5	Detmold
44G5	Dangriga	41K3	Detroit
22G3	Danilovskaya Vozvyshennost' reg.	21K2	Deva
22F4	Dankov	16C4	Deventer
44G6	Danli	43C2	Devils Gate pass
23D6	Danube r.	43C3	Devils Peak mt
41L4	Danville	13F6	Devizes
50C3	Daoukro	13C5	Devon r.
27H3	Da Qaidam	39J2	Devon Island i.
28E2	Daqing	35K7	Devonport
26B3	Dar'ā	23E7	Devrez r.
26D4	Dārāb	27F4	Dewas
21M4	Dardanelles str.	12F4	Dewsbury
52D4	Dar es Salaam	28C3	Deyang
20D2	Darfo Boario	26C3	Dezful
28C2	Darhan	28D3	Dezhou
46C2	Darién, Golfo del	26D4	Dhahran
27G4	Darjeeling	27H4	Dhaka
36D2	Darling r.	26C5	Dhamar
35K4	Darling Downs reg.	27G4	Dhanbad
34D5	Darling Range h.	27F5	Dhārwād
12F3	Darlington	11M7	Dhaulagiri mt
16H3	Darłowo	27F4	Dhule
16D6	Darmstadt	52E3	Dhuusa Mareeb
51E1	Darnah	21L7	Dia i.
13D7	Dart r.	43B3	Diablo, Mt mt
13H6	Dartford	43B3	Diablo Range mts
13C7	Dartmoor reg.	49D2	Diamantina
39M5	Dartmouth	35J3	Diamantina r.
12F4	Darton	47K6	Diamantina, Chapada plat.
15C3	Darty Mts h.	49A1	Diamantino
12E4	Darwen	47J6	Dianópolis
34G1	Darwin	50C3	Diapaga
48C8	Darwin, Mte mt	52C4	Dibaya
26D2	Dashkhovuz	27H4	Dibrugarh
54C6	Dassen Island i.	40F2	Dickinson
30H2	Datong	18E2	Dieppe
28D2	Datong	16D7	Dietikon
29E6	Datu Piang	38H3	Diffa
22C3	Daugava r.	26B4	Dibbagh, J. ad mt
11U9	Daugavpils	36G2	Dubbo
18G4	Dauphiné r.	41K5	Dublin
29E6	Davao	15E4	Dublin
29E6	Davao Gulf b.	22F3	Dubna
41H3	Davenport	23C5	Dubno
13J5	Daventry	21H3	Dubrovnik
55H3	Daveyton	11S9	Dubysa r.
45H7	Davis	24K3	Dudinka
43B2	Davis Strait str.	13E5	Dudley
16D7	Davos	50B4	Duékoué
38F4	Dawson Creek	19C2	Duero r.
18D5	Dax	14E5	Dufftown
28C3	Daxian	16D4	Duisburg
28C3	Daxue Shan mts	55G5	Dukathole
43D3	Daylight Pass	28C4	Dukou
26C3	Dayr az Zawr	48D3	Dulce r.
41K4	Dayton	41H2	Duluth
41K6	Daytona Beach	40F4	Dumas
30C7	Dazaifu	14D5	Dumbarton
54F5	De Aar	14E5	Dumfries
51F1	Dead Sea l.	21M4	Dumyât
13J6	Deal	16H7	Dunajská Streda
13E6	Dean, Forest of	17J7	Dunakeszi
48D4	Deán Funes	21N2	Dunării, Delta
38H3	Dease Strait chan.	17J7	Dunaújváros
43D3	Death Valley v.	40G5	Duncansby Head hd
21J4	Debar	14E2	Duncansby Head hd
17K7	Debrecen	15E3	Dundalk
52D2	Debre Markos	15E4	Dundalk Bay b.
52D3	Debre Zeyit	14F4	Dundee
41J4	Decatur	55J4	Dundee
41J5	Decatur	15F3	Dundonald
27F5	Deccan plat.	15F3	Dundrum Bay b.
16G5	Děčín	27G6	Dungarpur
49C4	Dedo de Deus mt	14E4	Dunfermline
50C3	Dédougou	15E3	Dungannon
13D4	Dee r.	52C3	Dungu
13C4	Dee r.	29C6	Dungun
15C3	Deel r.	14E2	Dunnet Head hd
15E3	Deele r.	13G6	Dunstable
16F6	Deggendorf	37B6	Dunstan Mts mts
21L6	Dej	14B3	Dunvegan, Loch b.
41J3	De Kalb	15E4	Durack r.
40D4	Delano Peak mt	18G4	Durance r.
41K3	Delaware	18G5	Durance r.
42D2	Delaware r.	44C3	Durango
42D3	Delaware r.	40F4	Durango
42D3	Delaware Bay b.	40F4	Durango div.
18E2	Delémont	16H4	Durban
18B4	Delft	55J4	Durban
30D5	Delfzijl	18F4	Durban-Corbières
27F4	Delhi	20B6	Durbalah
27J4	Delhi	12F3	Durham
43D5	Delnys	41L4	Durham
43D5	Del Mar	12F3	Durham
25E2	Delmenhorst	16H4	Durankulak
38B3	De Long Mts mts	23F6	Dokuchayev's'k
19E1	Demanda, Sierra de la mts	18G2	Dole

16F6	Domažlice	26E3	Dushanbe
16J7	Dombóvár	23H7	Dushet'i
45M5	Dominica	16C5	Düsseldorf
45K5	Dominican Republic	50C3	Dutse
20C1	Domodossola	28C4	Duyun
48B5	Domuyo, Volcán mt	26E4	Düzce
14F3	Don r.	26E4	Dwarka
23F5	Don r.	41J4	Dyat'kovo
19D3	Don r.	13D5	Dyersburg
12F4	Doncaster	39H2	Dyfi r.
15C3	Donegal b.	40B2	Dzhau Tau mt
23F6	Donets'k	22G3	Dzhankoy
23F5	Donets'kyy Kryazh h.	26E2	Dzhezkazgan
27J5	Dongfang	25P4	Dzhugdzhur, Khrebet mts
29D7	Donggala	24J5	Dzhungarskiy Alatau, Khr. mts
27J5	Đông Hôi	24H5	Dzhusaly
28D4	Dongting Hu l.	17K2	Działdowo
28D3	Dongying	22F4	Dzuunmod
43B2	Donner Pass pass	22C3	Dzyarzhynsk
21L6	Donoussa i.		
22F4	Donskoy		**E**
15B5	Doonbeg r.	39N4	Eagle
14D5	Doon, Loch l.	43D4	Eagle Crags mt
20B2	Dora Baltea r.	40F6	Eagle Pass
13E7	Dorchester	38D3	Eagle Plain plain
18E4	Dordogne r.	31H4	Eai-gawa r.
16B5	Dordrecht	14E4	Earn r.
50B3	Dori	14D4	Earn, L. l.
54C5	Doring r.	13H7	Easebourne
13G6	Dorking	37G2	East Cape c.
14C5	Dornoch Firth est.	28E3	East China Sea
17N7	Dorohoi	13H5	East Dereham
34C4	Dorre i.	6	Easter Island i.
16C5	Dortmund	55G5	Eastern Cape div.
50C3	Dosso	51F2	Eastern Desert
41J5	Dothan	27F5	Eastern Ghats mts
18J1	Douai	48E8	East Falkland i.
18B1	Douala	16C4	East Frisian Is
43C4	Double Peak mt	13G6	East Grinstead
18H3	Doubs r.	42E1	Easthampton
37A6	Doubtful Sound in.	14D5	East Kilbride
40E5	Douglas	13J7	Eastleigh
41K5	Douglas	14B3	East Loch Tarbert b.
12C3	Douglas	55G6	East London
49C2	Dourada, Cach.	39L4	Eastmain r.
49C1	Dourada, Serra mts	42D2	Easton
49A3	Dourados	43D1	East Range mts
49A3	Dourados r.	25Q2	East Siberian Sea
19B2	Douro r.	29E7	East Timor terr.
13F4	Dove r.	14C2	East Walker r.
13J5	Dove r.	41H3	Eau Claire
13J7	Dover	44E4	Ebano
42D3	Dover	13D6	Ebbw Vale
13J7	Dover, Strait of	50D4	Ebebiyin
15F3	Downpatrick	16F4	Eberswalde-Finow
30D5	Dōzen i.	30H2	Ebetsu
49B3	Dracena	21L2	Eboli
16C4	Drachten	50D4	Ebolowa
21L2	Drăgăşani	32E1	Ebro r.
21H5	Draguignan	42C1	Ech Chélif
55H5	Drakensberg mts	38C3	Echo Bay b.
55J2	Drakensberg mts	19E1	Echternach
50C1	Dra, Oued r.	19D4	Écija
11M7	Drammen	16D3	Eckernförde
11M7	Drau r.	46C4	Ecuador
16H7	Drava r.	14F1	Eday i.
16F5	Dresden	51F3	Ed Damazin
18C2	Dreux	51F3	Ed Damer
21K2	Drobeta-Turnu Severin	51F3	Ed Dueim
23B5	Drohobych	50D4	Edéa
13E5	Droitwich	49C2	Edéia
13F4	Dronfield	12E3	Eden r.
39Q2	Dronning Louise Land reg.	21K4	Edessa
27F1	Drosh	40G6	Edinburg
41M2	Drummondville	14E5	Edinburgh
14D4	Drumochter Pass	16G7	Edirne
34F2	Drysdale r.	38G4	Edmonton
26D4	Dubai	39M5	Edmundston
38H3	Dubawnt Lake l.	21M5	Edremit
16H7	Dubrovnik	36E3	Edward r.
13G6	Dumdan	52C4	Edward, Lake l.
		40F5	Edwards Plateau
		43A1	Eel r.
		54D3	Eenzaamheid Pan
		41J4	Effingham
		17K7	Eger
		15E4	Egglish
		10F4	Egilsstaðir
		37D3	Egmont, Cape c.
		37E3	Egmont, Mt volc.
		21N5	Eğrigöz Daği mts
		49D1	Eguas r.
		51F2	Egypt
		30D7	Ehime
		16D6	Ehingen (Donau)
		14B4	Eigg i.
		26E6	Eight Degree Channel
		34E2	Eighty Mile Beach
		16F4	Eildon, Lake l.
		14C4	Eilean Shona i.
		16E5	Eindhoven
		16D7	Einsiedeln
		46E5	Eirunepé
		53E3	Eiseb r.
		16E5	Eisenach
		16G4	Eisenhüttenstadt
		17J7	Eisenstadt
		36E3	Edward r.
		13G6	Edenbridge
		21M4	Ergene r.
		50B2	El Iguidi
		15E3	Eriboll, Loch in.
		13G6	Ericht, Loch l.
		42A1	Erie
		41K3	Erie, Lake l.
		14A3	Eriskay i.
		52D2	Eritrea
		16E6	Erlangen
		55H3	Ermelo
		21L6	Ermoupoli
		27F5	Erode
		51D3	Erongo div.
		54A1	Er Rachidia
		50B1	El Bayadh
		50C1	Erromango i.
		21J4	Ersekë
		36F4	Erzgebirge mts
		26C3	Erzincan
		26D3	Erzurum
		43D5	El Cajon
		46F2	El Callao
		40C5	El Centro
		19F3	Elche
		35H1	Elcho I. i.
		50C3	Elda
		52D3	Eldoret
		12D3	Esk r.
		11P7	Eskilstuna
		26B3	Eskişehir
		12D1	Feltre
		21L6	Esmeraldas
		28D2	Fengzhen
		51C1	El Bayadh
		16D4	Elbe r.
		40E4	Elbert, Mount mt
		17J3	Elbląg
		23G7	Elbrus mt
		26C3	Elazığ
		42C3	El Banco
		21J4	Elbasan
		50C1	El Bayadh
		16D4	Elbe r.

20C6	El Kala		**F**
40G4	El Khârga	20E3	Fabriano
43B2	Elk Grove	50C3	Fada-Ngourma
41J3	Elkhart	20D2	Faenza
50B2	El Khnâchîch	49C1	Fafen Shet' r.
40C3	Elko	21K2	Făgăraş
39H2	Ellef Ringnes I. i.	38D3	Fairbanks
40B2	Ellensburg	43A2	Fairfield
13D5	Ellery, Mt mt	14G1	Fair Isle i.
39K2	Ellesmere Island i.	41H3	Fairmont
37D5	Ellesmere, Lake l.	42A3	Fairmont
12E4	Ellesmere Port	38E4	Fairweather, Mt mt
13G4	Ellesmere	27F3	Faisalabad
38H3	Ellice r.	13D7	Fal r.
51F1	El Mansûra	14E5	Falkirk
50C1	El Meghaïer	48E8	Falkland Islands terr.
40F6	El Minya	48D8	Falkland Sound chan.
42C1	Elmira	42F2	Fall River
50B2	El Mreyyé reg.	13B7	Falmouth
16D4	Elmshorn	44J5	Falmouth
46D3	El Nevado, Cerro mt	40D2	False Bay b.
50C1	El Obeid	11M9	Falster i.
50C1	El Oued	17N7	Fălticeni
40E5	El Paso	11O6	Falun
19C4	El Prat de Llobregat	15E4	Fane r.
19C4	El Puerto de Santa María	28E2	Fangzheng
44G4	El Reno	14C4	Fannich, Loch l.
44C4	El Salto	20B2	Fano
44G6	El Salvador	20E3	Fano
20C6	El Tarf	13F7	Fareham
46E2	El Tigre	37A4	Farewell, Cape c.
46C1	El Tocuyo	37D4	Farewell Spit spit
23H5	El'ton, Ozero l.	13G6	Faringdon
51F2	El Tur	13G6	Farnborough
19C3	Elvas	12F2	Farne Islands is
33G3	Émaé i.	13G6	Farnham
11O8	Eman r.	50A2	Faro
24G5	Emba	18F3	Faro
55H3	Embalenhle	10-	Faroe Islands terr.
52D4	Embu	23H5	Fastiv
43C2	Excelsior Mts mts	50A3	Fatick
16C4	Emden	20E6	Favignana, Isola i.
55J2	eMijindini	13F7	Fawley
51O3	Emi Koussi mt	51D3	Faya
21M3	Eminska Planina h.	42F2	Fayetteville
16C4	Emmen	41J5	Fayetteville
16D7	Emmen	44E1	Fayetteville
40F6	Emory Pk mt	15B5	Feale r.
44B3	Empalme	40C2	Feather, Mt mt
55J4	Empangeni	18C2	Fécamp
20D3	Empoli	38F3	Federal
55H3	Emzinoni	37A6	Federal
31F6	Ena-san mt	46E3	Feijó
44A2	Encantada, Co de la mt	27F1	Feijó
48E3	Encarnación	52E3	Feira de Santana
43D5	Encinitas	24G2	Feldberg mt
36B3	Encounter Bay b.	16D6	Feldkirch
49E1	Encruzilhada	16G7	Feldkirchen in Kärnten
32E3	Endeavour Strait	49D2	Felixlândia
42C1	Endicott	13J6	Felixstowe
38B3	Endicott Mts mts	16D7	Fehrenfeld
23H5	Engel's	12D1	Feltre
29C7	Enggano i.	13G5	Fens, The reg.
13G5	England div.	13G6	Fenny
13H1	English Channel	28D2	Fengzhen
23G7	Enguri r.	24C1	Fenstanton
40G4	Enid	50D4	Fenoarivo Atsinanana
30H2	Eniwa	24G2	Feodosiya
51F3	Ennedi, Massif mts	24J2	Fergana
15D4	Ennell, Lough l.	41H2	Fergus Falls
15C5	Ennis	39N5	Ferkéssédougou
15D3	Enniskillen	55G2	Ferkéssédougou
16G7	Enns r.	21G6	Fermanagh
16C4	Enschede	15D3	Fermo
44A2	Ensenada	20E3	Fermoy
28C3	Enshi	15C5	Fernandina, Isla i.
19B3	Entroncamento	16C3	Fernandópolis
50C4	Enugu	13D7	Ferndown
46D5	Envira	40D2	Ferrara
46D5	Envira r.	20D2	Ferrara
37C5	Enys, Mt mt	19B1	Ferrol
31G6	Enzan	19D4	Ferreira
13H6	Epping	50C1	Fès

14-	Fetlar i.		**G**
47H3	French Guiana terr.	52E3	Gaalkacyo
21H4	Fier r.	43C2	Gabbs Valley Range mts
19B2	Figueira da Foz	45J2	Gaborone
19H1	Figueres	36G4	Gabon
33H3	Figuig	53C6	Gaborone
40D2	Filadélfia	21L3	Gabrovo
11T7	Estonia	50A3	Gabú
19C2	Estrela, Serra da mts	41J5	Gadsden
19E3	Estrella mt	20E4	Gaeta
18F2	Étampes	20E4	Gaeta, Golfo di g.
55J3	eThandukukhanya	50C1	Gafsa
52D3	Ethiopia	22E4	Gagarin
14C4	Etive, Loch in.	50B4	Gagnoa
20F6	Etna, Monte volc.	23G7	Gagra
26D4	Firûzâbâd	50A3	Gaiab r.
13J6	Frinton-on-Sea	40G5	Gainesville
39M3	Frobisher Bay b.	41K6	Gainesville
31H4	Gassan volc.	41K5	Gainesville
41K4	Gaston	13G4	Gainsborough
19E4	Gata, Cabo de c.	35H5	Gairdner, Lake l.
22D3	Gatchina	14C4	Gairloch
39L5	Gatineau r.	54E3	Galana r.
27F5	Goa div.	14E5	Galashiels
55G3	Gauteng div.	21N2	Galaţi
35J2	Flinders r.	50B4	Galana r.
19E2	Flensburg	50D1	Gala
15D3	Flores, Fumo	20F2	Galicia div.
14C3	Gascoyne r.	19C1	Galicia div.
34C3	Gascoyne r.	21K4	Giannitsa
50D3	Gashua	20C6	Galite, Canal de la chan.
50D4	Geel Vloer	20C6	Galite, Canal de la chan.
38H4	Geikie r.	18F3	Galle
21L4	Gökçeada i.	15B5	Galway
23E7	Gökirmak r.	15B4	Galway Bay g.
23D7	Gölcük	14C5	Gigha i.

(Remaining columns continued in the same index format — entries including Geelong, Gela, Gelendzhik, Gelsenkirchen, Gemena, General Acha, General Alvear, General Belgrano, Geneva, Genoa, Gent, George, Georgetown, Georgia, Geraldton, Germany, Gerede, Germiston, Ghadāmis, Ghana, Ghardaïa, Ghazni, Gibraltar, Gibson Desert, Gifu, Gijón, Gila, Gilbert Islands, Gillingham, Gilroy, Gimbala, Girona, Gisborne, Glace Bay, Gladstone, Glasgow, Glass Mt, Glen Affric, Glen Coe, Glasnevin, Glencoe, Glendale, Glenelg, Glen Esk, Glen Garry, Glen More, Glen Nevis, Glenrothes, Glogów, Gloucester, Goa, Gobabis, Godavari, Gökova, Golden Gate, Goldsboro, Golmud, Goma, Gombe, Gondar, Good Hope Cape of, Gorakhpur, Gordon, Gori, Gorizia, Gorki, Görlitz, Gorontalo, Gosford, Gosport, Gotha, Gothenburg, Gotland, Gotō-rettō, Goulburn, Gouraya, Governador Valadares, Gower pen., Goya, Gozo, Graaff-Reinet, Grafton, Graham Island, Grampian Mountains, Granada, Gran Canaria, Grand Bahama, Grand Canyon, Grand Cayman, Grande, Grand Erg Occidental, Grand Erg Oriental, Grand Forks, Grand Junction, Grand Rapids, Grasse, Graz, Great Abaco, Great Australian Bight, Great Barrier Reef, Great Basin, Great Bear Lake, Great Dividing Range, Great Exuma, Great Falls, Great Inagua, Great Karoo, Great Salt Lake, Great Sandy Desert, Great Slave Lake, Great Victoria Desert, Greece, Greeley, Green Bay, Greenland, Greenock, Greensboro, Greenville, Greenwood, Grenada, Grenoble, Grey Range, Grimsby, Griqualand, Grombalia, Groningen, Groote Eylandt, Grootfontein, Grudziądz, Guadalajara, Guadalcanal, Guadalquivir, Guadalupe, Guadiana, Guaíra, Guaitecas, Islas — among others.)

Gualeguay r. 12F3
Guam terr. 42B1
Guamblin, I. i. 16D4
Guamúchil 42F2
Guanajato 11T6
Guanambi 16D4
Guanare 34D3
Guane
Guangyuan 28E3
Guangzhou 28B2
Guanhães 14D5
Guanhães r. 45M2
Guanipa r. 37E2
Guantánamo 39L5
Guaporé r. 41K4
Guará r. 43B3
Guarabira 16C5
Guarapari 50B2
Guarapuava
Guaraqueçaba 20D6
Guaratinguetá 51D1
Guarda
Guarujá 42D3
Guasave 42C4
Guassú r. 26D4
Guatemala 54E1
Guatemala
Guaviare r. 31H4
Guaxupé 14C2
Guayaquil 28D3
Guayaquil, Golfo de g. 43C3
Guayaramerin 28B2
Guaymas 28E3
Gubbio 28E3
Gubkin 16D4
Gudaut'a 1109
Gudbrandsdalen v. 29C4
Gudermes 28C3
Guelma 31H5
Guelmine 53D5
Guernsey i. 50A4
Guichen B. b. 28E2
Guider 48E1
Guidonia-Montecelio 11K6
Guiglo 54E2
Guildford 52E3
Guilin 52E3
Guimarães 17M7
Guinea
Guinea-Bissau
Guinea, Gulf of g. 30E6
Güines 40G6
Guiratinga 16B4
Guiyang 13H6
Gujarat div. 11P5
Gujranwala 5084
Gukovo 39L4
Gulbene 14B3
Gulfport 4282
Gulistan 4283
Gulrip'shi 14A3
Gulu 12F4
Gumdag 23F7
Gümüşhane 54D4
Guna 11K6
Gunma 42E2
Gunungsitoli 12F3
Gurgueia r. 11H8
Gurinhã 2882
Gurjaani 13J6
Gurupi r. 27F4
Gusau 35K7
Gusev 13G6
Gus'-Khrustal'nyy 17M7
Guspini 27F5
Güstrow 16B5
Gütersloh 37F3
Guwahati 13H7
Guyana 40G3
Guzar 13H7
Gwadar 12G4
Gwalior 29C5
Gwanda 30D6
Gweebarra Bay b. 41J5
Gweru 52E3
Gwydir r. 11J7
Gyaring Co l. 37E3
Gyaring Hu l. 11V5
Gyaros i. 37E2
Gydanskiy Poluostrov pen. 37A7
Gympie 50B1
Gyöngyös 45H4
Gyula 13G7
Gyumri 16F4
Gyzylarbat 13C6

H
Haapsalu 11S7
Haarlem 16B4
Hachado, P. de 48C7
Hachinohe 30H3
Hachiōji 31G6
Hadano 31G6
Haderslev 11L9
Hadejia 50D3
Hadera 26B3
Haeju 28E3
Haeju-man b. 28E3
Hafnarfjörður 10B4
Hafursfjörður 10B4
Hagar Nish Plat. 51F3
Hagen 16C5
Hagerstown 42C3
Hagi 30C6
Haguenau 16D6
Hai Dương 28C4
Haifa 26B3
Haikou 28D5
Ha'il 26C4
Hailar 28E2
Hailsham 13H7
Hai Phong 28C4
Haiti 45J5
Haiwee Reservoir 43C3
Hajdúböszörmény 17K7
Hajhir mt 52D1
Hako-dake mt 30H3
Hakodate 30H3
Hakos Mts mts 54B1
Hakseen Pan 54D2
Haku-san volc. 31F5
Halâniyât, Juzur al i. 52D1
Halberstadt 16E5
Haldensleben 16E4
Halesowen 13E5
Halesworth 13J5
Halifax 12F4
Hallein 16F7
Halmahera i. 29F6
Halmstad 11N8
Hamada 30C6
Hamadān 26C3
Hamada Tounassine des. 50B2
Haricha des. 50B3
Hamamatsu 31G6
Hamar 11M6
Hamātah, Gebel mt 51F2
Hambantota 27G6

Hambleton Hills 16D7
Hamburg 48C9
Hamden 54J4
Hameln 48F3
Hamersley Range mts 13J6
Hämeenlinna 11L8
Hamhŭng 42C2
Hami 13G6
Hamilton 35L4
Hamilton 43D4
Hamilton 38E3
Hamilton 43B3
Hamilton 12E3
Hamilton 54C6
Hamilton, Mt mt 12E4
Hamilton 28D3
Hammamet 41H2
Hammamet, Golfe de b. 30J2
Hammond 44C3
Hammonton 49C2
Hampton 30D6
Hāmūn-e Jaz Mūriān 31H4
Hanahai r. 31E6
Hanamaki 3087
Handa Island i. 14C2
Handan 4083
Hanford 43C2
Hangayn Nuruu mts 41L4
Hangzhou 13G6
Hangzhou Wan b. 11S7
Hanko 26E3
Hannibal 30C7
Hannover 31F6
Hanöbukten b. 29C4
Ha Nôi 16D4
Hanover 28C3
Hanzhong 31H5
Haramachi 41K5
Harare 53D5
Harbin 2882
Harbours, B. of b. 27F3
Hardangervidda plat. 11K6
Hardap div. 54B3
Härer 52E3
Hargeysa 52E3
Harghita-Mădăraş, Vârful 17M7
Harima-nada b. 30E6
Harlingen 40G6
Harlow 13G6
Härnösand 11P5
Harney Basin 5084
Harricanaw r. 39L4
Harris 14B3
Harrisburg 42C2
Harrisonburg 42B3
Harris, Sound of chan. 14A3
Harrogate 12F4
Harşit r. 23F7
Harteigan mt 31G5
Hartford 42E2
Hartlepool 12F3
Härtsfeld h. 11H8
Har Us Nuur l. 2882
Harwich 13J6
Haryana div. 27F4
Hashima 50C4
Hashimoto 31G6
Hasselt 13G6
Hasselt 1685
Hastings 37F3
Hastings 40G3
Hastings 13H7
Hatfield 13G6
Ha Tinh 29C5
Hattiesburg 41J5
Haud r. 52E3
Hauhungaroa mt 37E2
Haukivesi l. 11V5
Hauraki Gulf g. 37E2
Haut Atlas mts 50B1
Hauts Plateaux 50B1
Havana 45H4
Havant 13G7
Havel r. 16F4
Haverfordwest 13C6
Havlíčkův Brod 16G6
Havre 40E2
Hawaiian Islands 6
Hawarden 13D4
Hawea, L. l. 37B6
Hawick 14F5
Hawke, P. de 3786
Hawke Bay b. 37F3
Haxby 12E3
Hayachine-san mt 31H4
Hayes r. 39J4
Hayes Halvø pen. 39M2
Haynes r. 39J3
Haysyn 23D5
Hayward 43A3
Haywards Heath 13G7
Hazelton 42D2
Heanor 13F4
Hecate Strait 38E4
Hechi 28C4
Hefei 28D3
Hegang 28F2
Heidelberg 16D6
Heidelberg 55H4
Heilbronn 16D6
Heilong Jiang r. 25O4
Hekla volc. 10D4
Helagsfjället mt 10N5
Helen, Mt mt 40D2
Helensburgh 14D4
Helgoländer Bucht b. 16C4
Hellín 19F3
Helmond 16B5
Helmsdale r. 14E2
Helmstedt 16E4
Helsingborg 11N8
Helsingør 11N8
Helsinki 11T6
Helvellyn mt 12E3
Hemel Hempstead 13G6
Henares r. 19E2
Hendek 23D7
Henderson 41J4
Hendon 41H5
Hengduan Shan mts 2884
Hengelo 16C4
Hengyang 28D4
Heniches'k 23E6
Henley-on-Thames 13G6
Henzada 29B5
Herāt 26E3
Hérault r. 18F5
Hereford 13E5
Hereford 40F5
Herford 16D4

Herisau 13G7
Hermite, Is i. 28C1
Hermosillo 55J4
Hernandarias 36F4
Herne Bay 33J1
Herning 16D5
Hershey 14E2
Hertford 13G6
Hervey Bay b. 35L4
Hess r. 43D4
Hetch Hetchy Aqueduct canal 43B3
Hetton 12E3
Hettstedt 16D4
Heywood 12E4
Heze 28D3
Hidaka-sanmyaku mts 30J2
Hidalgo del Parral 44C3
Hidrolândia 49C2
Higashi-Hiroshima 31H4
Higashine 31E6
Higashi-ōsaka 3087
Higashi-suidō chan. 30C7
Hikone 31F6
Hildesheim 16D4
Hilton Head I. 41K5
Hilversum 16B4
Himachal Pradesh div. 27F3
Himalaya mts 30E6
Himare 31H4
Himeji 31H4
Himi 31F5
Hims 2683
Hinchinbrook I. i. 35X2
Hinckley 13F5
Hindley 46F5
Hindmarsh, L. l. 36C4
Hindu Kush mts 26E3
Hinnøya i. 1002
Hirado 3087
Hirakata 30D6
Hiratsuka 31G6
Hirosaki 30H3
Hiroshima 30D6
Hiroshima 30D6
Hirschberg mt 16E7
Hispaniola i. 45K4
Hīt 21K2
Hitachi 17J7
Hitachi-ōta 31H5
Hitoyoshi 30C7
Hjälmaren l. 1107
Hjørring 11M8
Hlotse 55H4
Hlukhiv 23E5
Ho 50C4
Hobart 35K7
Hobbs 40F5
Hobro 11L8
Hô Chí Minh 29C5
Hochschwab mt 16G7
Hodder r. 12E4
Hoddesdon 13G6
Hódmezővásárhely 17K7
Hof 16E5
Hofsjökull ice cap 10D4
Höfu 30C6
Hoggar plat. 53C5
Hohhot 16F7
Hoh Xil Shan mts 28A3
Hoima 52D3
Hokianga Harbour 37D1
Hokitika 31G5
Hōki-gawa r. 30D6
Hokkaidō 30J2
Hokkaidō 30J1
Hokuriku Tunnel 31E6
Holbæk 11M9
Holguín 45J4
Hollister 43B3
Holešov 43B3
Hollywood 41K6
Holstebro 11L8
Holston r. 41K4
Holyhead 13C4
Holy Island i. 12F2
Holy Island i. 13C4
Holyoke 42E1
Holywell 13D4
Home Bay b. 39M3
Homyel' 23D4
Honda 31H4
Hondo 30D6
Honduras 44G6
Hongjiang 27J4
Hong Kong div. 29D4
Hông, Sông r. 28C4
Hongze Hu l. 2883
Honiara 33F2
Honjō 31H4
Honshū i. 30D6
Hood, Mt volc. 4082
Hoogeveen 16C4
Hoorn 16B4
Hope 37D5
Hope Saddle pass 42C4
Hopewell 43F2
Hopkins, L. l. 34F3
Horizon Depth 33J4
Horki 30D6
Horlivka 23E5
Horn r. 26D4
Horn, Cape c. 48C9
Hornavan l. 10D6
Horn, Isles de is 33J3
Horoshiri-dake mt 30J2
Horqin Youyi Qianqi
Horsens 11L9
Horsham 13G6
Horsham 38F3
Horton r. 17N5
Hosa'ina 52D3
Hoshiarpur 27F3
Hoste, I. i. 48C9
Hotagen l. 1005
Hotan 49E1
Hotham, Mt mt 38F4
Hot Springs 44F2
Hotte, Massif de la mts 45K5
Houghton le Spring 12F3
Houma 41H6
Houma 14C3
Houston 41G6
Hout r. 55H1
Houtman Abrolhos is 34C4
Hovd 28B2

Hove 13G7
Hövsgöl Nuur l. 28C1
Howick 55J4
Howitt, Mt mt 36F4
Howland Island i. 33J1
Höxter 16D5
Hoy i. 14E2
Hoyerswerda 16G5
Höytiäinen l. 10V5
Hradec Králové 16G5
Hrasnica 21H3
Hsipaw 27H4
Huacho 28E2
Huachi 28D2
Huaibei 28D3
Huainan 28D3
Huallaga r. 46C5
Huambo 53B5
Huancayo 13F5
Huang He r. 12F4
Huangshan 28D4
Huangshan Gaoyuan plat. 28D3
Huánuco 46C5
Huanuni 46E7
Huarmey 46C5
Huascaran, Nevado de mt 46C5
Huasco r. 4883
Huatabampo 44C3
Hubli 27F5
Hucknall 13F4
Huddersfield 12F4
Hudson Bay b. 39K4
Hudson Land reg. 3902
Hudson Strait str. 39L3
Huê 29C5
Huehuetenango 44C3
Huelva 19C4
Huesca 19F1
Huhudi 54F3
Huiarau Range mts 37F3
Huib-Hoch Plateau plat. 54B3
Huich'ŏn 28E2
Huila, Nevado de volc. 31G5
Huixtla 44F5
Hulin 10L2
Humaitá 12H4
Humber, Mouth of the est. 12H4
Humenné 17K6
Humphreys, Mt 43C3
Humphreys Peak 40D4
Húnaflói b. 10C4
Hunchun 21K2
Hunedoara 17J7
Hungary 41J3
Hüngnam 2506
Hunte r. 16D4
Hunter r. 36H2
Hunter I. i. 33H4
Huntingdon 13G5
Huntington 41K4
Huntington Beach 43C3
Huntsville 39L5
Huntsville 41G5
Huntsville 41G5
Hurghada 51F2
Huron 40G3
Huron, Lake l. 41K3
Hurunui r. 21N4
Huş 4382
Husum 39L2
Huzhou 28E3
Hvannadalshnúkur mt 10C4
Hvar i. 20G3
Hvita r. 10C4
Hwange 53C5
Hyderabad 27F6
Hyderabad 26D7
Hyères 18H5
Hyères, Îles d' is 18H5
Hyesan 15D2
Hyōgo 30E6
Hyōnosen mt 30E6
Hythe 13J6
Hyūga 31E6
Hyvinkää 11T6

I
Ijebu-Ode 50C4
Íjssel r. 1684
Ijsselmeer l. 1684
Ikageng 55J4
Ikaria i. 21M6
Ikast 30B7
Iki i. 17J4
Ilagan 52C4
Ilām 26C3
Ilapel 50C4
Ilebo 52C4
Ilford 13H6
Ilfracombe 13C6
Ilha Grande, Baía da b. 49D3
Ilhavo 19B2
Ilhéus 49E1
Ilkeston 13F5
Ilkley 12F4
Illapel 4884
Iller r. 16E7
Illichivs'k 23D6
Illimani, Nevado de mt 46E7
Illinois r. 41H4
Illinois div. 41J4
Illintsi 23D5
Illizi 50C2
Il'men', Ozero l. 22D3
Ilo 46D7
Iloilo 29E5
Ilorin 50C4
Ilovays'k 23F6
Ilovlya r. 39K4
Imabari 30D6
Imaichi 31G5
Imari 3087
Imatra 11V6
Imbituba 4883
Imbituva 4984
Imola 20D2
Imperatriz 47J5
Imperia 20C3
Imperial Beach 43D5
Impfondo 52B3
Imphal 27H4
Ina 49D2
Ina-gawa r. 31G6
Inambari r. 46E6
Inanwatan r. 29E1
Inari 10U2
Inarijärvi l. 10T2
Inawashiro 31H5
Inazawa 31H5
Inca 19H3
Inch'ŏn 28E2
Incomati r. 55X2
Indaal, Loch in. 12A5
Indaiá r. 49D2
Indaiá Grande r. 49E2
Indalsälven r. 10P5
Independence 41H4
Inderborskiy 24G5
Indian r. 27H4
Indiana 42D2
Indiana div. 41J3
Indianapolis 41J4
Indianola 34C1
Indian Ocean 41H5
Indianola 41H5
Indigirka r. 25Q2
Indija 21J2
Indonesia 29D7
Indore 49E3
Indre r. 18E3
Indre r. 26F3
Indus, Mouths of the est. 26D7
Inegöl 21N4
Ingalls, Mt mt 43B2
Inglefield Land reg. 39L2
Ingolstadt 16E6
Ingushskaya Respublika div. 23H7
Inhaca, Península 55X3
Inhambane 55X2
Inhambane div. 55X1
Inhandavá r. 15A4
Inishark i. 15A4
Inishbofin i. 15A4
Inishmaan i. 15A4
Inishmore i. 15A4
Inishowen pen. 15D2
Inishturk i. 15A4
Inland Kaikoura Range mts 37D5
Inner Sound chan. 14C3
Innoshima 16E6
Innsbruck 16E7
Inny r. 13H4
Inongo 52B4
Inowrocław 16J4
In Salah 50C2
Inscription, C. c. 34C4
Inta 24H3
Inuvik 38E3
Invercargill 37E4
Inverness 14D3
Inveruno r. 35H6
Investigator Strait 36H3
Inyo Mts mts 43C3
Ioannina 21J5
Iona i. 12A5
Ionian Islands is 20G6
Ionian Sea 21L6
Ios i. 21L6
Iowa div. 40G3
Iowa Falls 41H3
Iowa City 41H3
Ipameri 49C2
Ipatinga 49D2
Ipatovo 23G7
Ipelegeng 55J3
Ipiales 46C3
Ipiranga 49B4
Ipoh 28C6
Ipojuca r. 47L5
Iporá 49B2
Ippy 52C3
Ipswich 35L4
Ipswich 13H5
Iput' r. 39M3
Iqaluit 21H7
Iquique 21L7
Iquitos 46D4
Iraklia i. 21L7
Iramaia 49E1
Iran 19D3
Irapuato 44D4
Irati 49B4
Irbid 26D3
Irbit 24H4
Irece 47K6
Ireland, Rep. of 15D4
Irian Jaya reg. 29F7
Iringa 53D4
Irira r. 49E1
Iriri r. 47J4
Irish Sea 12B4
Irkutsk 25M4
Irosin 29B5
Irpin' 23D5
Irrawaddy r. 27H4
Irrawaddy, Mouths of the est. 27G5
Irthing r. 12E3
Irtysh r. 24J4

Irún 19F1
Irvine 14D5
Irvine 43D5
Isabela 29E6
Isabela, Isla i. 46
Isabela, Cordillera mts 45G6
Isafjarðardjúp est. 10B3
Ísafjörður 10B3
Isahaya 30C7
Isakogorka 22G1
Isalo, Massif de l' mts 53E6
Ísere r. 20E4
Isernia 20F4
Isesaki 31G6
Ise-wan b. 30H2
Iseyin 50C4
Ishikari-gawa r. 30H2
Ishikari-wan b. 30H2
Ishikawa 31H4
Ishinomaki 31H5
Ishinomaki-wan b. 31H5
Ishioka 31H5
Isikveren 21J2
Isil'kul' 24J4
Isipingo 55C3
Isiro 52C3
Iskenderun 24K4
Iskur r. 21L3
Islamabad 27F3
Island Lagoon 35H5
Islands, Bay of b. 37E1
Islay 14B5
Isla Isabel i. 51F1
Isola di Capo Rizzuto 20G5
Israel 26B3
Isiolo r. 50B4
Issyk-Kul' l. 26A2
İstanbul 21L4
Istra pen. 46F6
İstres 18G5
Itabaianinha 47L6
Itaberaba 47K6
Itabira 49D2
Itaberito 49D3
Itabuna 31G6
Itacoatiara 47G4
Itaeté 49C3
Itaí 49D3
Itaituba 47G4
Itajaí 48E3
Itajaí 49D3
Italy 20F4
Itamarandiba 49E2
Itambacuri 49E2
Itambé, Pico de mt 49D2
Itanguari r. 49D1
Itanhaém r. 42B4
Itanhém r. 49E2
Itapajipe 49C2
Itaparica, Ilha i. 49C3
Itapebi 47K5
Itapecuru Mirim 47L6
Itapemirim 49E2
Itaperuna 49E2
Itapetinga 47K5
Itapetininga 49C3
Itapeva 49C3
Itapicuru r. 47K5
Itapicuru r. 47L6
Itapicuru Mirim 47L4
Itapipoca 49E1
Itaquari 49C3
Itararé 49C3
Itárema r. 45K5
Ithaca 42C1
Itimbiri r. 52C3
Itinga 49E2
Itiquira r. 49A2
Itoigawa r. 31G6
Itoigawa 31E5
Itu 49C3
Ituiutaba 49C2
Itumbiara 49C2
Ituporanga 47J5
Iturama 49C2
Iturup, Ostrov i. 2505
Ituxi r. 46D4
Itzehoe 16D4
Ivai r. 48B3
Ivalo 10U2
Ivalojoki r. 10U2
Ivanava 22G3
Ivanhoe 36F2
Ivano-Frankivs'k 23C5
Ivanovo 22G3
Ivanovo Oblast' div. 22G3
Ivdel' 24H3
Ivindo r. 49B3
Ivinheima 49B3
Ivinheima r. 2082
Ivrea 20B2
Ivris Ugheltekhili pass 24K3
Iwaki 31H5
Iwaki-san volc. 30H3
Iwakuni 30C6
Iwamizawa 30H2
Iwanuma 31H4
Iwasuge-yama volc. 31F6
Iwate 31H4
Iwate-san volc. 31H4
Iwo 50C4
Ixmiquilpan 44E4
Iyo 30D7
Iyomishima 30D7
Izbica 16H4
Izberbash 23H7
Izhevsk 24G4
Izhma 22K1
Izhma r. 22K1
İzmir 21K5
İzmir Körfezi g. 21K5
Izobil'nyy 23G6
İzra 21H6
Izu-hantō pen. 31G6
Izumi 30C7
Izumo 30D6
Izu-Shotō is 31G6

J
Jagdalpur 27G5
Jaguaraíva 49C4
Jahrom 26D4
Jaipur 27F4
Jajce 20G2
Jakarta 29C7
Jalal-Abad 26E3
Jalandhar 27F3
Jalapa Enriquez 43D4
Jalgaon 49B3
Jalingo 50D4
Jalna 27F4
Jalpaiguri 27G4
Jamaica 45J5
Jamaica Channel 45J5
Jamanxim r. 47G5
Jambi 29C7
James r. 42B4
James r. 40G2
James Bay b. 39K4
James Island reg. 3902
Jamestown 16C7
Jamestown 42C2
Jamestown 42B1
Jammu 27F3
Jammu and Kashmir terr. 27F3
Jamshedpur 27G4
Janaúba 49D1
Janesville 41J3
Januária 49D1
Japan 28F3
Japan, Sea of 31E4
Japurá r. 46E4
Japurá r. 49A3
Jardim 48J4
Jardines de la Reina, Archipiélago de los is 45H4
Jarocin 16H5
Jarosław 17L5
Järpen 11T6
Järvenpää 11T6
Jason Is is 48D8
Jastrzębie-Zdrój 17J6
Jászberény 17J7
Jataí 4982
Jatapu r. 47G4
Jaú 49C3
Jaú r. 46F4
Jauru r. 49B2
Java i. 29C7
Java i. 52C4
Java Sea 29D7
Jawhar 52E3
Jaya, Pk mt 29F7
Jaya, Pk mt 49E2
Jayapura 29G7
Jaz'air Farasān is 51E3
Jebel Abyad Plat. 2684
Jedeida 20C6
Jefferson r. 41H4
Jefferson, Mt mt 43D2
Jejuí Guazú r. 48E2
Jēkabpils 1118
Jelenia Góra 11S8
Jelgava 29D7
Jember 16E5
Jena 16E5
Jendouba 41H5
Jennings 41H5
Jequié 49E1
Jequitaí 49D2
Jequitaí r. 49D2
Jequitinhonha 49E1
Jequitinhonha r. 49E2
Jérémie 45J5
Jerez de la Frontera 19C4
Jersey i. 18C2
Jersey City 42D2
Jerumenha 47K5
Jerusalem 2683
Jervis B. b. 36H3
Jervis Bay Terr. 36H3
Jesenice 20F1
Jesi 20E3
Jessup r. 41K5
Jesús María 48D4
Jhansi 27F4
Jiamusi 28F2
Ji'an 28E3
Jianyang 2883
Jiayuguan 28B3
Jihlava 16G6
Jijiga 52E3
Jilib 52E3
Jima 52D3
Jiménez 44D3
Jinan 28D3
Jingdezhen 28D3
Jingmen 28D3
Jinhua 28D4
Jining 28D3
Jining 28D2
Jinja 52D3
Jinotepe 44G6
Jinzhou 28E2
Jiparaná r. 46F5
Jipijapa 46B4
Jishou 28C4
Jixi 28F2
João Pessoa 47M5
João Pinheiro 49C2
Job Peak mt 43C2
Jodhpur 27F4
Joensuu 10V5
Jōetsu 31G5
Jõgeva 11U7
Jõhvi 11U7
Joinville 48J3
Jõkulsá á Brú r. 10F4
Jõkulsá á Fjöllum r. 10E3
Jökulsá í Fljótsdal 10F4
Joliet 41J3
Joliette 41M2
Jolo 29E6
Jonava 11T9
Jonesboro 41H4
Jones Sound chan. 39K2
Jongleí Canal 51F4
Jönköping 1108
Jonquière 39L5
Joplin 41H4
Jordan 2683
Jordão r. 49B4
Jorhat 27H4
Jos 50D4
Joseph Bonaparte Gulf 34F1
Jos Plateau plat. 50C4
Jouberton 55G3

Joyce's Country reg. 15B4
Juan de Fuca, Strait of chan. 40B2
Juàzeiro 47K5
Juàzeiro do Norte 47L5
Juba 51F4
Jubba r. 52E3
Jubilee Pass pass 43D4
Júcar r. 19F3
Juchitán 44E5
Jucururu r. 49E2
Judenburg 16G7
Juist i. 16C5
Juiz de Fora 49D3
Juliaca 46D7
Julio, 9 de 48D5
Julijske Alpe mts 19F3
Jumilla 2684
Junagadh 26F4
Junction City 41G4
Jundiaí 49C3
Juneau 38E4
Jungfrau mt 16C7
Juniata r. 42C2
Junipero Serro Peak mt 43B3
Juquiá 49C4
Jur r. 51E4
Jura mts 18H3
Jura i. 14C4
Jura, Sound of chan. 14C5
Jurbarkas 11S9
Jūrmala 11S8
Juruena r. 46F6
Jutaí i. 46E4
Jutiapa 44G6
Juticalpa 44G6
Juventud, Isla de la i. 45H4
Jwaneng 53C6
Jyväskylä 11T5

K
K2 mt 27F3
Kabale 52C4
Kabalo 52C4
Kabardino-Balkarskaya Respublika div. 23H7
Kapiti I. 37E4
Kabongo 52C4
Kābul 26E3
Kabwe 53C5
Kachchh, Gulf of 26E4
Kaçkar Dağı mt 23G7
Kadavu Passage chan. 26A2
Kadıköy 21H7
Kadmat i. 27E5
Kadoma 53C5
Kaduqli 51E3
Kaduna 50C4
Kaduna r. 50C4
Kaédi 50A3
Kaélé 50D3
Kaesŏng 28E3
Kaffrine 50A3
Kafue 53C5
Kafue r. 53C5
Kaga 31F5
Kaga Bandoro 52B3
Kagawa 30E6
Kagoshima 23D5
Kaharlyk 23D5
Kahayan r. 29D7
Kaherekoau Mts 37A6
Kahraman Maraş 2683
Kai Besar i. 29F7
Kai Kecil i. 29F7
Kaimanawa 37E2
Kaimur Range h. 27G4
Kainan 31E6
Kaipara Harbour 37D1
Kairouan 50D1
Kaiyuan 28C4
Kakata 50A4
Kakamega 52D3
Kakanui Mts mts 37C6
Kakegawa 31G6
Kakhovka 23E6
Kākināda 27G5
Kakogawa 30E6
Kakuda 31H5
Kalaå Kebira 20D7
Kalabo 53C5
Kalach 23G5
Kalach-na-Donu 23G6
Kalahari Desert 54D1
Kalak r. 21K4
Kalamaria 21K4
Kalamazoo 41J3
Kalaus r. 23G6
Kalémié 52C4
Kalgoorlie 34E5
Kalima 52C4
Kaliningrad 11S9
Kaliningradskaya Oblast' div. 11S9
Kalinkavichy 23D5
Kalispell 40D2
Kalisz 16J5
Kalitva r. 23G5
Kalix 10S3
Kalixälven r. 10U3
Kalkaska 41K3
Kallavesi l. 10U5
Kallsjön l. 11P8
Kalmar 11P8
Kalmarsund chan. 11P8
Kalmykiya, Respublika div. 23H6
Kaluga 22F4
Kalundborg 11M9
Kalush 23C5
Kalutara 27G6
Kama r. 24G4
Kamaishi 31H4
Kamakura 31G6
Kamamaung 27H5
Kamchatka 25R4
Kamchatka Pen. 25R4
Kamchiya r. 21M3
Kamen'-na-Obi 24J4
Kamenka 23G5
Kamensk-Shakhtinsky 23G5
Kamensk-Ural'skiy 24H4
Kamet mt 27F3
Kamień Pomorski 16G4
Kamieskroon 54C3
Kamina 52C4
Kaminoyama 31H5
Kamloops 38G4
Kamogawa 31G6
Kampala 52D3
Kampong Cham 29C5
Kâmpóng Chhnăng 29C5

Kâmpóng Spoe 29C5
Kâmpóng Thum 29C5
Kâmpôt 29C5
Kamuli 52D3
Kam'yanets'-Podil's'kyy 23C5
Kamyshin 23H5
Kanash 22H4
Kanawha r. 41K4
Kanazawa 31G5
Kanchipuram 27F5
Kandalaksha 10X3
Kandi 50C3
Kandy 27G6
Kane Basin b. 39M2
Kanevskaya 23G6
Kangar 29C6
Kangaroo I. i. 36A3
Kangchenjunga 27G4
Kepulauan 29D7
Kangnŭng 28E3
Kanin, Poluostrov pen. 22J1
Kankakee 41J3
Kankan 50B3
Kannapolis 41K4
Kano 50C3
Kan-onji 30D6
Kanpur 27G4
Kansas r. 40G4
Kansas div. 40G4
Kansas City 41H4
Kanto-sanchi mts 31G6
Kanuma 31G5
KaNyamazane 55J2
Kanye 53C6
Kao-hsiung 29E4
Kaokoveld plat. 53A5
Kaolack 50A3
Kapchagay 24J5
Kapiri Mposhi 53C5
Kapit 29D7
Kaposvár 16H7
Kapuas r. 29D7
Kapuskasing 39K5
Kapuvár 16G7
Kara r. 24H3
Kara-Bogaz Gol, Zaliv b. 26D2
Karabük 23F7
Karacabey 21H4
Karachayevo-Cherkesskaya Respublika div. 23G7
Karachayevsk 23G7
Karachev 22F4
Karachi 26E4
Karaganda 24J5
Karaginskiy Zaliv 2554
Karakelong i. 29E6
Karakol 27F3
Karakoram Range mts 27F3
Karaman 23D5
Karamea Bight b. 37C4
Karamürsel 21N4
Karas r. 5483
Karasu 23E6
Karas div. 54B3
Karatau, Khr. mts 24H5
Karatsu 30C7
Karcag 17K7
Karditsa 21J5
Kárdla 11S7
Karesuando 10S2
Kargil 27F3
Kariba 53C5
Kariba-yama volc. 30G2
Karikachi Pass 30J2
Karikari, Cape c. 37D1
Karimata, Selat str. 29C7
Karis 11S6
Karkar I. i. 29G7
Karkinit's'ka Zatoka g. 23E6
Karlık Dağı mt 28A3
Karlova 23G5
Karlovac 20F2
Karlovy Vary 16F5
Karlshamn 11P9
Karlskrona 11P9
Karlsruhe 16D6
Karlstad 11N7
Karmøy i. 11L7
Karnal 27F4
Karnataka div. 27F5
Karnobat 21M3
Karpathou, Steno str. 21M6
Karpathos i. 21M6
Karratha 34C3
Kars 24G4
Karshi 26F3
Karskiye Vorota, Proliv str. 24G2
Kartal 21N4
Kartaly 24H4
Karwar 27F5
Kasai r. 52B4
Kasama 53D5
Kasanga 53D4
Kasane 53C5
Kasangulu 5081
Kasaragod 27F5
Kaseda 30C8
Kasempa 53C5
Kasese 52D3
Kashan 26D3
Kashi 24J6
Kashihara 30E6
Kashima 31H6
Kashima-nada b. 31H6
Kashin 22F3
Kashiwa 31G6
Kashiwazaki 31G5
Kāshmar 26D3
Kasimov 22G4
Kasli 24H4
Kasongo 52C4
Kasongo-Lunda 52B4
Kaspi 24G4
Kaspiysk 23H7
Kassala 51F3
Kassándras, Kólpos b. 21K4
Kassel 16D5
Kastamonu 23E7
Kastoria 21J4

Kasuga 30C7
Kasugai 30G7
Kasulu 52D4
Kasur 27F3
Katahdin, Mt mt 41N2
Katerini 21K4
Katha 27H4
Kathmandu 27G4
Kati 50A3
Katihar 27G4
Katiola 50B3
Katoomba 36H2
Katowice 17J5
Katrineholm 11P7
Katsina 50C3
Katsuta 31H5
Katsuura 31H6
Katsuyama 30C7
Kattakurgan 24H6
Kattegat str. 11M8
Kauai i. 1159
Kaura-Namoda 50C3
Kavadarci 21K4
Kavala 21L4
Kavir, Dasht-e des. 26D3
Kawagoe 31G6
Kawaguchi 31G6
Kawanishi 31G6
Kawhia Harbour 37E2
Kawkareik 27H5
Kaya 50B3
Kayanza 52C4
Kayes 50A3
Kayseri 2683
Kayyerkan 25L3
Kazakhskiy Melkosopochnik reg. 24J4
Kazan' 22H4
Kazanka r. 22H4
Kazakhstan 24H5
Kazanlŭk 21L3
Kazincbarcika 17K6
Kazuno 31H3
Kéa i. 21L6
Kebnekaise mt 10S3
Kebri Dehar 52E3
Kecskemét 17J7
Kédainiai 11S9
Kédougou 50A3
Keetmanshoop 54C2
Kefallonia i. 21J5
Keflavík 10B4
Keighley 12F4
Keila 11T7
Keitele l. 10U5
Kelang 29C6
Kelkit r. 23F7
Kelmė 11S9
Kelowna 38G5
Keluang 29C6
Kem' 22F1
Kemerovo 24K4
Kemi 10T4
Kemijoki r. 10T3
Kemp, Land reg. 57
Kempsey 36H2
Kempten (Allgäu) 16E7
Kempton Park 55H3
Kenai Mts mts 38C4
Kendal 12E3
Kendari 29E7
Kenema 50A4
Kenge 52B4
Kenhardt 54D3
Kénitra 50B1
Kennebec r. 41N2
Kennedy r. 35J2
Kennet r. 13F6
Kenneth r. 41J5
Kenosha 41J3
Kent div. 13H6
Kentucky r. 41K4
Kentucky div. 41K4
Kenya 52D3
Kenya, Mt mt 52D4
Keokuk 41H3
Keppel Bay b. 35L3
Kerala div. 27F6
Kerang 36E3
Kerava 11T6
Kerch 23F6
Kerchens'ka r. 23F6
Kerema 29G7
Keren 51F3
Kerguelen Islands 9
Kericho 52D4
Kerinci, G. volc. 29C7
Kerkyra 21J5
Kerma 51F3
Kermadec Islands 33J6
Kerman 26D3
Kermānshāh 26C3
Keros i. 21L6
Kerzhenets r. 22H3
Kesagami Lake l. 41K1
Kesennuma 31H4
Kestenga 10X4
Keszthely 16H7
Keta 50C4
Ketapang 29D7
Kętrzyn 17K4
Kettering 13G5
Kettle, Lough l. 15C3
Key Largo 41K7
Keynsham 13E6
Key West 41K7
Kgalagadi div. 54E2
Kgomofatshe Pan 54E1
Kgoro Pan 54E2
Khabarovsk 25P4
Khairpur 26E4
Khakassiya, Respublika div. 24K4
Khalkhāl 26C3
Khambhat, Gulf of g. 26F4
Khamir 52C1
Khammam 27G5
Khamra r. 25M3
Khanabad 27F2
Khanka, Lake l. 30D2
Khanty-Mansiysk 24H3
Kharabali 23H6
Kharagpur 27G4
Kharkiv 23F5
Khartoum 51F3
Khasavyurt 23H7
Khashm el Girba 51F3
Khashuri 23G7
Khaskovo 21L4
Khatanga, Gulf of 25M2
Khayelitsha 54C3
Khemis Miliana 19H4
Khenchela 50C1
Khenifra 50B1
Kherson 23E6
Kheta r. 25L2
Khmel'nyts'kyy 23D5
Khmelita 23D5
Khmis r. 54D2
Khodzheyli 26E2
Khokhowe Pan 54D1
Khomas Highland reg. 54B1
Khoni 23G7

Khoper r. 23G5
Khor 25P5
Khor r. 28F2
Khorramābād 26C3
Khorugh 26F3
Khrebet Dzhagdy 28E1
Khroma r. 25Q4
Khromtau 24G4
Khrystynivka 1706
Khŭjand 26E2
Khulna 55G3
Khust 23B5
Khutsong 55G3
Khyber Pass pass 26F3
Kičevo 21J4
Kidderminster 13E5
Kidnappers, Cape 37F3
Kidsgrove 13E4
Kiel 16E3
Kielce 17K5
Kieler Bucht b. 16E3
Kiev 23D5
Kiffa 50A3
Kifisia 21K5
Kigali 52D4
Kigoma 52C4
Kii-sanchi mts 31E6
Kii-suidō chan. 30E7
Kikinda 21J2
Kikuchi 32E2
Kikwit 52B4
Kilbrannan Sound chan. 14C5
Kilimanjaro mt 52D4
Kiliya 23D6
Kilkeel 15F3
Kilkenny 15D5
Killala Bay b. 15B3
Killarney 15A5
Killeen 40G5
Kilmarnock 14D5
Kil'mez' r. 22J3
Kilwinning 14D5
Kimberley Plateau 34E2
Kimberley 54F4
Kimch'aek 28E2
Kimhae 3086
Kimi 21L5
Kimolos i. 21L6
Kimovsk 22F4
Kimpoku-san mt 31G4
Kimry 22F3
Kinabalu, Gunung mt 29D6
Kinaros i. 21M6
Kindia 50A3
Kineshma 22G3
Kingaroy 35L4
King Leopold Ranges h. 34E2
Kingman 40D4
Kings r. 43C3
Kingsbridge 13D7
King's Lynn 13H5
Kingsmill Group is 33H2
King Sound b. 34D2
Kings Peak mt 40D3
Kingsport 41K4
Kingston 35K7
Kingston 39L5
Kingston upon Hull 12G4
Kingsville 40G6
Kingswood 13E6
King William I. i. 39J3
King William's Town 55G6
Kinshasa 52B4
Kintampo 50B4
Kintyre, Mull of 14C5
Kinyeti mt 51F4
Kipushi 53C5
Kiqu r. 25M4
Kiribati 33I2
Kirinyaga mt 52D4
Kirkağaç 21M5
Kirkby 13E4
Kirkby in Ashfield 13F4
Kirkcaldy 14E4
Kirkintilloch 14D5
Kirkland Lake 39K5
Kirklareli 21M4
Kirk Michael 12C3
Kirov 22F4
Kirovo-Chepetsk 22J3
Kirovohrad 23E5
Kirovsk 10X3
Kirovskaya Oblast' div. 22J3
Kirriemuir 14E4
Kirthar Range mts 26E4
Kiruna 10S3
Kiryū 31G5
Kisangani 52C3
Kiselevsk 24K4
Kishinev 23D6
Kishiwada 30E6
Kiskunfélegyháza 17J7
Kiskunhalas 17J7
Kislovodsk 23G7
Kismaayo 52E3
Kiso-gawa r. 30H2
Kiso-sanmyaku mts 30G7
Kissidougou 50A4
Kita 50B3
Kitakami 31H4
Kitakami r. 31H4
Kitakata 31G5
Kitakyūshū 30C7
Kitale 52D3
Kitami 30J2
Kitchener 41K3
Kitgum 52D3
Kitimat 38F4
Kitinen r. 10U3
Kittilä 10T3
Kitwe 53C5
Kitzbüheler Alpen mts 16E7
Kivik 11N8
Kivu, Lake l. 52C4
Kizel 24G4

São José dos Campos
São José dos Pinhais
São Lourenço
São Lourenço r.
São Luís
São Manuel
São Marcos r.
São Mateus
São Mateus r.
São Miguel r.
Saône r.
São Nicolau i.
São Paulo
São Paulo div.
São Raimundo Nonato
São Romão
São Sebastião do Paraíso
São Sebastião, Ilha de i.
São Simão
Sao-Siu
São Tiago i.
São Tomé i.
Sao Tome and Principe
São Tomé, Cabo de c.
São Vicente
São Vicente i.
São Vicente, Cabo de c.
Sapporo
Saqqez
Sarāb
Sara Buri
Sarajevo
Sarandë
Saransk
Sarapul
Sarasota
Saratov
Saratovskaya Oblast' div.
Saravan
Saravan
Sarawak div.
Sarca r.
Sardinia i.
Sarektjåkkå mt
Sar-e Pol
Sarh
Sārī
Saria i.
Sarıkamış
Sarīr Tibesti des.
Sarıyer
Sarkand
Sarnen
Sarnia
Sarny
Saronikos Kolpos g.
Saros Körfezi b.
Sarova
Sarpsborg
Saru-gawa r.
Sarumasa-yama mt
Sárvár
Saryozek
Sasebo
Saskatchewan r.
Saskatchewan div.
Saskatoon
Sasolburg
Sasovo
Sassandra
Sassari
Satpura Range mts
Satsunai-gawa r.
Satte
Satu Mare
Sauðárkrókur
Saudi Arabia
Sault Ste Marie
Sault Ste Marie
Saumur
Saurimo
Sava r.
Savala r.
Savalou
Savannah
Savannah r.
Savannakhét
Savanna la Mar
Save r.
Savoie reg.
Savona
Savonlinna
Sawatch Range mts
Sawu Sea g.
Sayḩūt
Saynshand
Sayoa mt
Sbeitla
Scafell Pike mt
Scalpay i.
Scalpay i.
Scapa Flow in.
Scarba i.
Scarborough
Scarborough
Scarborough
Scarp i.
Schaffhausen
Schelde r.
Schenectady
Schiehallion mt
Schio
Schleswig
Schönebeck
Schwäbisch Hall
Schwandorf
Schwarzenberg
Schwarzrand mts
Schwaz
Schwedt
Schweinfurt
Schwenningen
Schwerin
Schwyz
Sciacca
Scilly, Isles of is
Scioto r.
Scoresby Land reg.
Scoresby Sund chan.
Scotland div.
Scottsbluff
Scranton
Scridain, Loch in.
Scunthorpe
Seaford
Seal r.
Searcy
Seaside
Seattle
Sebastián Vizcaíno, Bahía b.
Sebeş
Sechura
Sechura, Bahía de b.
Secretary Island i.
Secunda
Secunderabad
Sedan
Sédhiou
20B6 Sédrata
50A4 Sefadu
29C6 Segamat
22E2 Segezha
50B3 Ségou
19D2 Segovia
19G2 Segre r.
50B4 Séguéla
40G6 Seguin
19F3 Segura r.
10S1 Seiland i.
10S5 Seinäjoki
18E2 Seine r.
18D2 Seine, Baie de b.
18F2 Seine, Val de v.
29C7 Sekayu
31F6 Seki
50B4 Sekondi
12F4 Selby
53C6 Selebi-Phikwe
24J4 Seletyteniz, Ozero l.
50A3 Sélibabi
22E3 Seliger, Oz. l.
39J4 Selkirk
44G2 Selma
43C3 Selma
13G7 Selsey Bill hd
46D4 Selvas reg.
38E3 Selwyn Mts
35H3 Selwyn Range h.
29D7 Semarang
22H3 Semenov
23G6 Semikarakorsk
23F5 Semiluki
24K4 Semipalatinsk
26D3 Semnān
23G7 Senaki
46E5 Sena Madureira
30C8 Sendai
31H4 Sendai
30C8 Sendai-gawa r.
50A3 Senegal
50A3 Sénégal r.
16G5 Senftenberg
52D4 Sengerema
47K6 Senhor do Bonfim
20E3 Senigallia
10P2 Senja i.
18F2 Senlis
31E6 Sennan
55G5 Senqu r.
18F2 Sens
44G6 Sensuntepeque
21J2 Senta
49D3 Sepetiba, Baía de b.
32E2 Sepik r.
39M4 Sept-Îles
29E7 Seram i.
29F7 Seram Sea g.
21J3 Serbia div.
23H4 Serdoba r.
23H4 Serdobsk
29C6 Seremban
22H4 Sergach
22F3 Sergiyev Posad
21L6 Serifos i.
24H4 Serov
53C6 Serowe
22F4 Serpukhov
21K4 Serres
47L6 Serrinha
49D2 Sêrro
49C3 Sertãozinho
22D2 Sertolovo
29D7 Seruyan r.
20E4 Sessa Aurunca
20C2 Sestri Levante
22D2 Sestroretsk
18F5 Sète
49D2 Sete Lagoas
11K7 Setesdal v.
50C1 Sétif
31F6 Seto
30D7 Seto-naikai
50B1 Settat
19B3 Setúbal
19B3 Setúbal, Baía de b.
39J4 Seul, Lac l.
23E6 Sevastopol'
13H6 Sevenoaks
13E6 Severn r.
39J4 Severn r.
22G2 Severnaya Dvina r.
23H7 Severnaya Osetiya, Respublika div.
25M1 Severnaya Zemlya is
24H3 Severnyy
28D1 Severo Baykalskoye Nagorye mts
22F1 Severodvinsk
10X2 Severomorsk
24L3 Severo-Yeniseyskiy
46C3 Sevilla
19D4 Seville
21L3 Sevlievo
38B3 Seward Peninsula
40E6 Sextín r.
7 Seychelles
23E5 Seym r.
21L2 Sfântu Gheorghe
50D1 Sfax
14C3 Sgurr Mor mt
27G4 Shahdol
26D3 Shahr-e Kord
26E3 Shakhrisabz
23G6 Shakhty
22H3 Shakhun'ya
28B3 Shaluli Shan mts
28C3 Shandan
28E3 Shandong Bandao pen.
53C5 Shangani r.
28E3 Shanghai
28D4 Shangrao
28E2 Shangzhi
15C5 Shannon r.
15C5 Shannon est.
15B5 Shannon, Mouth of the est.
28D4 Shaoyang
14F1 Shapinsay i.
23D5 Sharhorod
30K2 Shari-dake volc.
26D4 Sharjah
34C4 Shark Bay b.
42A2 Sharon
22H3 Shar'ya
53C6 Shashe r.
52D3 Shashemenē
28D3 Shashi
40B3 Shasta, Mt volc.
22F4 Shatura
42B3 Shavers Fork r.
42D2 Shawangunk Mts
41M2 Shawinigan
41G4 Shawnee
22F4 Shchekino
23F5 Shchigry
23F5 Shebekino
26E3 Sheberghān
39K5 Sheboygan
50D4 Shebshi Mts
15D4 Sheelin, Lough l.
13H6 Sheerness
13F4 Sheffield
25R3 Shelikhova, Zaliv g.
38C4 Shelikof Strait
43A1 Shell Mt mt
42B3 Shenandoah r.
42B3 Shenandoah Mts
28E2 Shenyang
23C5 Shepetivka
33G3 Shepherd Is is
36E4 Shepparton
13H6 Sheppey, Isle of i.
39L5 Sherbrooke
40E3 Sheridan
41G5 Sherman
16B5 's-Hertogenbosch
13F4 Sherwood Forest
24G5 Shetpe
40G2 Sheyenne r.
14B3 Shiant Islands is
31G5 Shibata
30K2 Shibetsu
30J1 Shibetsu
31G5 Shibukawa
14C4 Shiel, Loch l.
31E6 Shiga
27G2 Shihezi
28D3 Shijiazhuang
30D7 Shikoku i.
30D7 Shikoku-sanchi mts
12F3 Shildon
27G4 Shiliguri
27H4 Shillong
30C7 Shimabara
31G6 Shimada
30D6 Shimane
25O4 Shimanovsk
31G6 Shimizu
31G6 Shimoda
31G5 Shimodate
27F5 Shimoga
30C7 Shimonoseki
31G5 Shinano-gawa r.
55J1 Shingwedzi r.
31H4 Shinjō
14D2 Shin, Loch l.
31F5 Shinminato
30C6 Shin-nanyō
52D4 Shinyanga
31H4 Shiogama
31F5 Shiojiri
12F4 Shipley
31H5 Shirakawa
31G5 Shirane-san volc.
28F3 Shirane-san mt
26D4 Shīrāz
42E2 Shirley
31H5 Shiroishi
31G5 Shirone
27F4 Shivpuri
28D3 Shiyan
25M6 Shizuishan
31G6 Shizuoka
31G6 Shizuoka
21H3 Shkodër
30D6 Shōbara
30H2 Shokanbetsu-dake mt
43D2 Shoshone Mts
23E5 Shostka
23G6 Shpakovskoye
23D5 Shpola
41H5 Shreveport
13E5 Shrewsbury
26D2 Shubarkuduk
21M3 Shumen
22H4 Shumerlya
53D5 Shurugwi
22G3 Shuya
24H5 Shymkent
26E4 Şiahan Range mts
11S9 Šiauliai
55K3 Şibayi, Lake l.
20F3 Šibenik
29B7 Siberut i.
52B4 Sibiti
21L2 Sibiu
29B6 Sibolga
29D6 Sibu
52B3 Sibut
28C4 Sichuan Pendi basin
20E6 Sicilian Channel
20E6 Sicily i.
46D6 Sicuani
19H5 Sidi Aïssa
19G4 Sidi Ali
50B1 Sidi Bel Abbès
20C7 Sidi Bouzid
20D7 Sidi El Hani, Sebkhet de
50A2 Sidi Ifni
50B1 Sidi Kacem
14E4 Sidlaw Hills h.
13D7 Sidmouth
41K5 Sidney Lanier, L.
26B3 Sidon
49A3 Sidrolândia
18F5 Sié, Col de pass
17L4 Siedlce
16D5 Siegen
20D3 Siena
17J5 Sieradz
48C6 Sierra Grande
50A4 Sierra Leone
44D5 Sierra Madre del Sur mts
43C4 Sierra Madre Mts
44C3 Sierra Madre Occidental mts
44D3 Sierra Madre Oriental mts
40B3 Sierra Nevada mts
43B2 Sierra Nevada mts
40D5 Sierra Vista
16C7 Sierre
21L6 Sifnos i.
19F5 Sig
17L7 Sighetu Marmaţiei
17M7 Sighişoara
29B6 Sigli
50B3 Siguiri
29C5 Sihanoukville
26C3 Siirt
29C7 Sijunjung
27F4 Sikar
50B3 Sikasso
41J4 Sikeston
25P5 Sikhote-Alin' mts
21L6 Sikinos i.
27G4 Sikkim div.
19C1 Sil r.
11S9 Šilalė
44D4 Silao
20C6 Siliana
27G3 Siling Co l.
21M2 Silistra
21N4 Silivri
11O6 Siljan l.
11L8 Silkeborg
11U7 Sillamäe
11R9 Šilutė
40E5 Silver City
15C5 Silvermine Mts h.
43D3 Silver Peak Range
42C3 Silver Spring
29D6 Simanggang
21N5 Simav Dağları mts
42A1 Simcoe
39L5 Simcoe, Lake l.
52D2 Simēn Mountains
29B6 Simeuluë i.
23E6 Simferopol'
43C4 Simi Valley
16D7 Simplon Pass pass
35H4 Simpson Desert
43D2 Simpson Park Mts
51F2 Sinai reg.
40E6 Sinaloa div.
20D3 Sinalunga
46C2 Sincelejo
14E2 Sinclair's Bay b.
16D6 Sindelfingen
50B4 Sinfra
29C6 Singapore
29C6 Singapore
52D4 Singida
29C6 Singkawang
36H2 Singleton
20C4 Siniscola
20G3 Sinj
21N2 Sinoie, Lacul lag.
26B2 Sinop
28E2 Sinŭiju
16J7 Siófok
16C7 Sion
41G3 Sioux City
41G3 Sioux Falls
28E2 Siping
45H6 Siquia r.
11K7 Sira r.
35H2 Sir Edward Pellew Group is
43C4 Sirretta Peak mt
27F4 Sirsa
51D1 Sirte
51D1 Sirte, Gulf of g.
11T9 Širvintos
20G2 Sisak
43B4 Sisquoc r.
55J3 Siteki
49D1 Sítio do Mato
13H6 Sittingbourne
29B4 Sittwe
26B3 Sivas
18G5 Six-Fours-les-Plages
55H2 Siyabuswa
23E6 Skadovs'k
10D3 Skagafjörður in.
11M8 Skagen
11L8 Skagerrak str.
11L8 Skanderborg
17K5 Skarżysko-Kamienna
17J6 Skawina
38F4 Skeena r.
13H4 Skegness
10R4 Skellefteå
10Q4 Skellefteälven r.
12E4 Skelmersdale
21K5 Skiathos i.
12D3 Skiddaw mt
11L7 Skien
17K5 Skierniewice
50C1 Skikda
12E4 Skipton
11L8 Skive
10E4 Skjálfandafljót r.
15F6 Skokholm Island
13B6 Skomer Island i.
21K5 Skopelos i.
22F4 Skopin
21J4 Skopje
11N7 Skövde
43D3 Skull Peak mt
11R8 Skuodas
23D5 Skvyra
14B3 Skye i.
21L5 Skyros i.
11M9 Slagelse
15E5 Slaney r.
22D3 Slantsy
20G2 Slatina
21L2 Slatina
38G4 Slave r.
50C4 Slave Coast
21H2 Slavonija reg.
21H2 Slavonski Brod
23C5 Slavuta
23F6 Slavyansk-na-Kubani
16H3 Sławno
14C3 Sleat pen.
14C3 Sleat, Sound of
15D5 Slieveardagh Hills
15C4 Slieve Aughty Mts
15C5 Slieve Bernagh h.
15D5 Slieve Bloom Mts
15B4 Slieve Gamph h.
15A5 Slieve Mish Mts
15D2 Slieve Snaght mt
15C3 Sligo
15C3 Sligo Bay b.
21M3 Sliven
21M2 Slobozia
22C4 Slonim
33F2 Slot, The chan.
13G6 Slough
17J6 Slovakia
20F1 Slovenia
20F1 Slovenj Gradec
23F5 Slov''yans'k
16H3 Słupsk
22C4 Slutsk
25M4 Slyudyanka
17N3 Smarhon'
21J2 Smederevo
21J2 Smederevska Palanka
23D5 Smila
43C1 Smoke Creek Desert
38G4 Smoky r.
40G4 Smoky Hills h.
10K5 Smøla i.
22E4 Smolensk
22E4 Smolenskaya Oblast' div.
21L4 Smolyan
10F4 Snæfell mt
40C2 Snake r.
40D3 Snake River Plain
16B4 Sneek
54F6 Sneeuberg mts
20F2 Snežnik mt
17K4 Śniardwy, Jezioro l.
14B3 Snizort, Loch b.
10N3 Snøtinden mt
13C4 Snowdon mt
36G4 Snowy r.
36G4 Snowy Mts mts
40F5 Snyder
53E5 Soanierana-Ivongo
14B3 Soay i.
51F4 Sobat r.
29G7 Sobger r.
30C7 Sobo-san mt
47K4 Sobral
23F7 Sochi
44C2 Socorro
49C3 Socorro
46D2 Socorro
44B5 Socorro, I. i.
26D5 Socotra i.
43D4 Soda Lake l.
11P7 Södertälje
52D3 Sodo
11Q6 Södra Kvarken str.
21K3 Sofia
11J6 Sognefjorden in.
51F2 Sohâg
18F2 Soissons
30D6 Sōja
23C5 Sokal'
26A3 Söke
23G7 Sokhumi
50C4 Sokodé
22G3 Sokol
17L4 Sokółka
17L4 Sokołow Podlaski
50C3 Sokoto
50C3 Sokoto r.
23C5 Sokyryany
27F5 Solāpur
13F7 Solent, The str.
13F5 Solihull
24G4 Solikamsk
24G4 Sol'-Iletsk
22F3 Solnechnogorsk
33G2 Solomon Islands
32F2 Solomon Sea
29E7 Solor, Kepulauan is
16C7 Solothurn
22E1 Solovetskiye Ostrova is
20G3 Šolta i.
14E6 Solway Firth est.
53C5 Solwezi
21M5 Soma
31H5 Sōma
52E3 Somalia
21H2 Sombor
41K4 Somerset
39J2 Somerset Island i.
54C7 Somerset West
11L9 Sønderborg
16E5 Sonderhausen
20C1 Sondrio
29C4 Sông Đa r.
53D5 Songea
29C6 Songkhla
52B4 Songo
53D5 Songo
29C4 Sơn La
49D2 Sono r.
47J6 Sono r.
44B3 Sonora r.
40D6 Sonora div.
44G6 Sonsonate
25S4 Sopka Shiveluch mt
51E4 Sopo r.
17J3 Sopot
16H7 Sopron
20E4 Sora
39L5 Sorel
19E2 Soria
23D5 Soroca
49C3 Sorocaba
24G4 Sorochinsk
29F7 Sorong
52D3 Soroti
10S1 Sørøya i.
19B3 Sorraia r.
29E5 Sorsogon
22D2 Sortavala
55H2 Soshanguve
23F4 Sosna r.
48C4 Sosneado mt
22K2 Sosnogorsk
11V7 Sosnovyy Bor
17J5 Sosnowice
23F6 Sosyka r.
45J8 Sotara, Volcán volc.
50B4 Soubré
50C1 Souk Ahras
28E3 Sŏul
51F1 Soûr
19H4 Sour el Ghozlane
38H5 Souris r.
47L5 Sousa
50D1 Sousse
54E4 South Africa, Republic of
13F7 Southampton
39K3 Southampton I.
42C4 South Anna r.
13F4 South Anston
35G4 South Australia div.
12F3 South Bank
41J3 South Bend
42E1 Southbridge
41K5 South Carolina div.
29D5 South China Sea
40F3 South Dakota div.
13G7 South Downs h.
55F2 South East div.
36F5 South East Cape
32E6 South East Cape
13H6 Southend-on-Sea
37C5 Southern Alps
38J4 Southern Indian Lake l.
34D6 Southern Ocean
14D5 Southern Uplands
14F4 South Esk r.
43A1 South Fork Eel r.
43C4 South Fork Kern r.
42B3 South Fork South Branch r.
48□ South Georgia i.
14A3 South Harris i.
42E2 Southington
37C6 South Island i.
43B2 South Lake Tahoe
42C2 South Mts h.
14□ South Nesting Bay b.
33H5 South Pacific Ocean
40F3 South Platte r.
12D4 Southport
14F2 South Ronaldsay i.
38G4 South Saskatchewan r.
12F2 South Shields
37E3 South Taranaki Bight b.
12E3 South Tyne r.
14A3 South Uist i.
37A7 South West Cape
55H1 Soutpansberg mts
20G5 Soverato
22B4 Sovetsk
28G2 Sovetskaya Gavan'
24H3 Sovetskiy
55G3 Soweto
17P4 Sozh r.
19E2 Spain
13G5 Spalding
45J5 Spanish Town
43C2 Sparks
45H2 Spartanburg
21K6 Sparti
20G6 Spartivento, Capo c.
28F2 Spassk-Dal'niy
35H5 Spencer Gulf est.
12F3 Spennymoor
15D3 Sperrin Mts
16D5 Speßart reg.
21K6 Spetses i.
14E3 Spey r.
16D6 Speyer
16C7 Spiez
16B5 Spijkenisse
20E1 Spilimbergo
17K6 Spišská Nová Ves
24C2 Spitsbergen i.
16F7 Spittal an der Drau
20G3 Split
40C2 Spokane
20E3 Spoleto
16G5 Spree r.
41H4 Springdale
40B3 Springfield
41K4 Springfield
41H4 Springfield
41J4 Springfield
42E1 Springfield
13J5 Sprowston
12H4 Spurn Head c.
20G5 Squillace, Golfo di g.
25R4 Sredinnyy Khrebet mts
21K3 Sredna Gora mts
25M3 Sredne-Sibirskoye Ploskogor'ye plat.
25N4 Sretensk
27G6 Sri Lanka
27F3 Srinagar
27F5 Srivardhan
16D4 Stade
16C4 Stadskanaal
14B4 Staffa i.
13E5 Stafford
13G6 Staines
23F5 Stakhanov
17L5 Stalowa Wola
13G5 Stamford
42E2 Stamford
55H3 Standerton
55J4 Stanger
21K3 Stanke Dimitrov
48E8 Stanley
12F3 Stanley
52C3 Stanley, Mount
25N4 Stanovoye Nagor'ye mts
25O4 Stanovoy Khrebet mts
17K5 Starachowice
22D3 Staraya Russa
21L3 Stara Zagora
16G4 Stargard Szczeciński
41J5 Starkville
16E7 Starnberger See l.
23F5 Starobil's'k
17J4 Starogard Gdański
23C5 Starokostyantyniv
23F6 Starominskaya
23F5 Staryy Oskol
42C2 State College
41K5 Statesboro
42B3 Staunton
11J7 Stavanger
13F4 Staveley
23G6 Stavropol'
23G6 Stavropol'skaya Vozvyshennost' reg.
23G6 Stavropol'skiy Kray div.
18C2 St-Brieuc
18G4 St-Chamond
18H2 St-Dié
18G2 St-Dizier
55J2 Steenkampsberge mts
40C3 Steens Mt mt
38H2 Stefansson I. i.
16E6 Steigerwald for.
10M4 Steinkjer
54C6 Stellenbosch
20C3 Stello, Monte mt
16E4 Stendal
14E4 Stenhousemuir
23H7 Step'anavan
36C2 Stephens r.
37D4 Stephens, Cape c.
40F3 Sterling
18G4 St-Étienne
42A2 Steubenville
13G6 Stevenage
38E3 Stewart r.
37A7 Stewart Island i.
33G2 Stewart Islands is
16G6 Steyr
13A6 St George's Chan.
18C2 St Helier
41M2 St-Hyacinthe
38E4 Stikine r.
44E1 Stillwater
21K4 Štip
14E4 Stirling
39L5 St-Jean, Lac l.
18D2 St-Lô
18C2 St-Malo
18C2 St-Malo, Golfe de
18D4 St-Médard-en-Jalles
18C3 St-Nazaire
18H2 St-Nicolas-de-Port
49C4 Sto Amaro, I. de
49D2 Sto Antônio r.
49E1 Sto Antônio de Jesus
49A1 Sto Antônio de Leverger
16H6 Stockerau
11Q7 Stockholm
13E4 Stockport
43B3 Stockton
12F3 Stockton-on-Tees
29C5 Stœng Trêng
13E4 Stoke-on-Trent
21G3 Stolac
13E5 Stone
49D1 Sto Onofre r.
11M9 Store Bælt chan.
11K6 Stornosa mt
42E2 Storrs
10O5 Storsjön l.
11L5 Storskrymten mt
10P4 Storuman l.
13E7 Stour r.
13F5 Stour r.
13J6 Stour r.
13J6 Stour r.
13E5 Stourbridge
13E5 Stourport-on-Severn
13H5 Stowmarket
18C2 St Peter Port
18G5 St-Pierre mt
18F2 St-Quentin
15D3 Strabane
20C2 Stradella
16F6 Strakonice
16F3 Stralsund
54C7 Strand
15F3 Strangford Lough l.
14C6 Stranraer
18H5 St-Raphaël
18H2 Strasbourg
13F5 Stratford-upon-Avon
14D3 Strathcarron v.
14D3 Strathconon v.
14D3 Strath Dearn v.
14D2 Strath Fleet v.
14D2 Strathnaver v.
14E2 Strath of Kildonan v.
14E3 Strathspey v.
16F6 Straubing
35G5 Streaky Bay b.
21K4 Strimonas r.
14E2 Stroma, Island of
20F5 Stromboli, Isola i.
14F1 Stronsay i.
13E6 Stroud
11L8 Struer
21J4 Struga
21K4 Struma r.
21K4 Strumica
21L3 Stryama r.
23B5 Stryy
22F4 Stupino
34F3 Sturt Creek r.
35J4 Sturt Desert des.
55G6 Stutterheim
16D6 Stuttgart
44F2 Stuttgart
17M5 Styr r.
49D2 Suaçuí Grande r.
21H1 Subotica
17N7 Suceava
15C4 Suck r.
46E7 Sucre
49B3 Sucuriú r.
23E6 Sudak
51F3 Sudan
39K5 Sudbury
13H5 Sudbury
51E4 Sudd swamp
16H5 Sudety mts
10□ Suðuroy i.
51E4 Sue r.
19F3 Sueca
51F2 Suez
51F1 Suez Canal canal
51F2 Suez, Gulf of g.
45J1 Suffolk
26D4 Şuḩār
28C1 Sühbaatar
16E5 Suhl
28F2 Suifenhe
28E2 Suihua
15D5 Suir r.
28D3 Suizhou
29C7 Sukadana
31H5 Sukagawa
22H2 Sukhona r.
26E4 Sukkur
30D7 Sukumo
11J6 Sula i.
26E3 Sulaiman Ranges
23H7 Sulak r.
29E7 Sula, Kepulauan is
29E7 Sulawesi i.
46B4 Sullana
20E3 Sulmona
41G5 Sulphur Springs
29E6 Sulu Archipelago
29D6 Sulu Sea
29B6 Şumatera i.
16F6 Šumava mts
29E7 Sumba i.
29D7 Sumba, Selat chan.
29D7 Sumbawa i.
53D4 Sumbawanga
53B5 Sumbe
14□ Sumburgh Head
14C2 Summer Isles is
43D2 Summit Mt mt
31G5 Sumon-dake mt
30E6 Şumoto
16H6 Šumperk
26C2 Sumqayıt
45H2 Sumter
23E5 Sumy
30H2 Sunagawa
14C4 Sunart, Loch in.
36E4 Sunbury
42C2 Sunbury
29C7 Sunda, Selat chan.
12F3 Sunderland
11P5 Sundsvall
29C7 Sungailiat
43A3 Sunnyvale
50B4 Sunyani
30C7 Suō-nada b.
22E2 Suoyarvi
41J2 Superior, Lake l.
26D4 Şūr
22H4 Šura r.
29D7 Surabaya
29D7 Surakarta
27F4 Surat
29B6 Surat Thani
24J3 Surgut
29E6 Surigao
29C5 Surin
47G3 Suriname
10C5 Surtsey i.
31G6 Suruga-wan b.
30D7 Susaki
42C2 Susquehanna r.
13F5 Sutton Coldfield
13F4 Sutton in Ashfield
33H3 Suva
22F4 Suvorov
31G5 Suwa
17L3 Suwałki
31G5 Suzaka
28D3 Suzhou
28E3 Suzhou
31F5 Suzu
31F6 Suzuka
10U1 Sværholthalvøya pen.
24C2 Svalbard terr.
23F5 Şvatove
11U9 Švenčionys
11M9 Svendborg
23F5 Sverdlovs'k
21J4 Sveti Nikole
23G6 Svetlograd
22B4 Svetlyy
10E4 Svíahnúkar volc.
21K2 Svinecea Mare, Vârful mt
22E2 Svir' r.
21L3 Svishtov
16H6 Svitava r.
16H6 Svitavy
23E5 Svitlovods'k
22J4 Sviyaga r.
25O4 Svobodnyy
21K3 Svrljiške Planine mts
23D4 Svyetlahorsk
13F5 Swadlincote
35L3 Swain Reefs rf
53B6 Swakopmund
12F3 Swale r.
13H6 Swanley
13D6 Swansea
13D6 Swansea Bay b.
55J3 Swaziland
11O6 Sweden
40F5 Sweetwater
40E3 Sweetwater r.
54D7 Şwellendam
16H5 Świdnica
16G4 Świdwin
16G4 Świebodzin
17J4 Świecie
38H4 Swift Current
15D2 Swilly, Lough in.
13F6 Şwindon
16G4 Świnoujście
16D7 Switzerland
15E4 Swords
22E2 Syamozero, Oz. l.
39M5 Sydney
36H2 Sydney
23F5 Syeverodonets'k
22J2 Syktyvkar
10N5 Sylarna mt
27H4 Sylhet
16D3 Sylt i.
21M6 Symi i.
23E5 Synel'nykove
20F6 Syracuse
41L3 Syracuse
24H5 Syrdar'ya r.
26B3 Syria
26B3 Syrian Desert des.
21M6 Syrna i.
21L6 Syros i.
22J2 Sysola r.
22J4 Syzran'
16G4 Szczecin
16H4 Szczecinek
17K4 Szczytno
17K7 Szeged
17J7 Székesfehérvár
17J7 Szekszárd
17K7 Szentes
20G1 Szigetvár
17K7 Szolnok
16H7 Szombathely

T

26D3 Ţabas
46E4 Tabatinga
49A2 Tabocó r.
16G6 Tábor
52D4 Tabora
50B4 Tabou
26C3 Tabrīz
26B4 Tabūk
33G3 Tabwémasana mt
11Q7 Täby
27G2 Tacheng
16F6 Tachov
29E5 Tacloban
46D7 Tacna
40B2 Tacoma
48E4 Tacuarembó
31G5 Tadami-gawa r.
50C2 Tademaït, Plateau du plat.
52E2 Tadjoura
51F1 Tadmur
28E3 Taegu
28E3 Taejŏn
13C6 Taf r.
48C3 Tafi Viejo
31H4 Tagajō
23F6 Taganrog
23F6 Taganrog, Gulf of
30C7 Tagawa
29E6 Tagbilaran
20E1 Tagliamento r.
19J4 Tagma, Col de pass
19B3 Tagus r.
50C2 Tahat, Mt mt
50C3 Tahoua
28D3 Tai'an
28D2 Taibus Qi
37C6 Taieri r.
28E4 T'ai-nan
49D1 Taiobeiras
28E4 T'ai-pei
29C6 Taiping
30J2 Taisetsu-zan mts
29E4 T'ai-tung
28E4 Taiwan
28D4 Taiwan Strait str.
28D3 Taiyuan
26C5 Ta'izz
44F5 Tajamulco, Volcano de volc.
20C7 Tajerouine
26F3 Tajikistan
31F6 Tajimi
29B5 Tak
31H5 Takahagi
30D6 Takahashi
30D6 Takahashi-gawa r.
30E6 Takamatsu
31F5 Takaoka
37E2 Takapuna
30E6 Takasago
31G5 Takasaki
31E6 Takatsuki
30D7 Takatsuki-yama mt
31F5 Takayama
31F6 Takefu
30D6 Takehara
30C7 Takeo
30C7 Taketa
29C5 Takêv
30H2 Takikawa
37A6 Takitimu Mts mts
27G3 Taklimakan Shamo des.
30C7 Taku
46B4 Talara
29E6 Talaud, Kepulauan is
19D3 Talavera de la Reina
36G2 Talbragar r.
48B5 Talca
48B5 Talcahuano
24J5 Taldykorgan
29E7 Taliabu i.
41K5 Tallahassee
11T7 Tallinn
23D5 Tal'ne
11S8 Talsi
38G3 Taltson r.
36D2 Talyawalka r.
50B4 Tamale
30C7 Tamana
30D6 Tamano
50C2 Tamanrasset
13C7 Tamar r.
50A3 Tambacounda
36F4 Tambo r.
36F4 Tamboritha mt
22G4 Tambov
22G4 Tambovskaya Oblast' div.
19B1 Tambre r.
19B2 Tâmega r.
27F5 Tamil Nadu div.
41K6 Tampa
11S6 Tampere
44E4 Tampico
36H1 Tamworth
13F5 Tamworth
52D4 Tana r.
31E7 Tanabe
10V1 Tanafjorden chan.
52D2 Tana, Lake l.
34G2 Tanami Desert
20C2 Tanaro r.
50B4 Tanda
48E5 Tandil
36D2 Tandou L. l.
50B2 Tanezrouft reg.
52D4 Tanga
52C4 Tanganyika, Lake
28A3 Tanggula Shan mts
27H3 Tanggula Shankou pass
50B1 Tangier
27G3 Tangra Yumco l.
28D3 Tangshan
28B3 Taniantaweng Shan mts
29F7 Tanimbar, Kepulauan is
29E6 Tanjay
29C7 Tanjungkarang Telukbetung
29C7 Tanjungpandan
29D6 Tanjungredeb
29D6 Tanjungselor
28B1 Tannu Ola, Khrebet mts
51F1 Tanta
50A2 Tan-Tan
44E4 Tantoyuca
52D4 Tanzania
28E2 Tao'an
20F6 Taormina
50B1 Taourirt
11T7 Tapa
44F6 Tapachula
47G4 Tapajós r.
46F5 Tapauá
46E5 Tapauá r.
27F4 Tāpi r.
37D4 Tapuaenuku mt
47G7 Taquarí r.
49C3 Taquaritinga
49B3 Taquaruçu r.
15D5 Tar r.
50D4 Taraba r.
29D6 Tarakan
14A3 Taransay i.
20G4 Taranto
20G4 Taranto, Golfo di
46C5 Tarapoto
37E4 Tararua Range
17P6 Tarashcha
46D5 Tarauacá
46E5 Tarauacá r.
37F3 Tarawera, Mt mt
24K5 Tarbagatay, Khrebet mts
18E5 Tarbes
25P5 Tardoki-Yani, Gora mt
35L5 Taree
21L2 Târgovişte
21K2 Târgu Jiu
17M7 Târgu Mureş
17N7 Târgu Neamţ
17N7 Târgu Secuiesc
46F8 Tarija
29F7 Tariku r.
27G3 Tarim Pendi basin
29F7 Taritatu r.
55F6 Tarka r.
24J3 Tarko-Sale
50B4 Tarkwa
29E5 Tarlac
18F4 Tarn r.
17M7 Târnăveni
17K5 Tarnobrzeg
17K5 Tarnów
50B1 Taroudannt
20D3 Tarquinia
19G2 Tarragona
51F1 Tarsus
48D2 Tartagal
23H7 Tärtär r.
11U7 Tartu
49E2 Tarumirim
30C8 Tarumizu
23H7 Tashir
26E2 Tashkent
37D4 Tasman Bay b.
35J7 Tasmania div.
37D4 Tasman Mts
35L6 Tasman Sea
50C2 Tassili du Hoggar plat.
50C2 Tassili n'Ajjer plat.
17J7 Tatabánya
24J4 Tatarsk
25Q4 Tatarskiy Proliv str.
22J4 Tatarstan, Respublika div.
31G6 Tateyama
31F5 Tate-yama volc.
26C4 Tathlīth, W. r.
29E7 Tat Mailau, G. mt
17J6 Tatry reg.
30E6 Tatsuno
49C3 Tatuí
26C3 Tatvan
47K5 Taua
49D3 Taubaté
29B4 Taung-gyi
13D6 Taunton
42F2 Taunton
37E3 Taupo, Lake l.
11S9 Tauragė
37F2 Tauranga
20G5 Taurianova
29B5 Tavoy
13C6 Taw r.
29D6 Tawau
13D6 Tawe r.
44E5 Taxco
14E4 Tay r.
14E4 Tay, Firth of est.
14D4 Tay, Loch l.
25L3 Taymura r.
25M2 Taymyr, Ozero l.
25L2 Taymyr, Poluostrov pen.
29C5 Tây Ninh
29D5 Taytay
24K3 Taz r.
50B1 Taza
19J4 Tazmalt
23H7 T'bilisi
23G6 Tbilisskaya
52B4 Tchibanga
51D2 Tchigaï, Plateau du plat.
17J3 Tczew
37A6 Te Anau, L. l.
44F5 Teapa
50C1 Tébessa
20B7 Tébessa, Monts de mts
48E3 Tebicuary r.
29B6 Tebingtinggi
20C6 Tébourba
20C6 Téboursouk
23H7 Tebulos Mt'a mt
43D5 Tecate
50B4 Techiman
44D5 Tecomán
17N7 Tecuci
26E3 Tedzhen
12F3 Tees r.
12E3 Teesdale reg.
46E4 Tefé r.
44G6 Tegucigalpa
43C4 Tehachapi
43C4 Tehachapi Pass
26D3 Tehrān
44F5 Tehuantepec, Golfo de g.
44F5 Tehuantepec, Istmo de isth.
13C5 Teifi r.
13D7 Teign r.
13D7 Teignmouth
43C4 Tejon Pass pass
44G4 Tekax
52D2 Tekezē Wenz r.
21M4 Tekirdağ
23H7 T'elavi
26B3 Tel Aviv-Yafo
49B4 Telêmaco Borba
21L2 Teleorman r.
43D3 Telescope Peak
47G5 Teles Pires r.
13E5 Telford
11S9 Telšiai
55H2 Temba
29C6 Tembelan, Kepulauan is
25L3 Tembenchi r.
55H3 Tembisa
13E5 Teme r.
43D5 Temecula
29C6 Temerloh
24J4 Temirtau
20C4 Tempio Pausania
41G5 Temple
23F6 Temryuk
48B5 Temuco
46C4 Tena
43D1 Tenabo, Mt mt
27G5 Tenali
29B5 Tenasserim
27H6 Ten Degree Chan.
31H4 Tendō
50D3 Ténéré reg.
50D2 Ténéré du Tafassâsset des.
50A2 Tenerife i.
19G4 Ténès
29D7 Tengah, Kepulauan is
26E1 Tengiz, Oz. l.
50B3 Tengréla
50B3 Tenkodogo
41J4 Tennessee r.
41J4 Tennessee div.
10U2 Tenojoki r.
44F5 Tenosique
19C3 Tentudia mt
49B3 Teodoro Sampaio
49E2 Teófilo Otôni
44D4 Tepatitlán
21J4 Tepelenë
44D4 Tepic
16F5 Teplice
19H1 Ter r.
20E3 Teramo
23H7 Terek r.
49A3 Terenos
22H4 Tereshka r.
47K5 Teresina
49D3 Teresópolis
23F7 Terme
26E3 Termez
20E6 Termini Imerese
20F4 Termoli
13E5 Tern r.
29E6 Ternate
20E3 Terni
23C5 Ternopil'
25Q5 Terpeniya, Zaliv g.
38F4 Terrace
20C5 Terralba
41J4 Terre Haute
23G5 Tersa r.
19F2 Teruel
20G2 Tešanj
52D2 Teseney
22G4 Tesha r.
30J2 Teshio-dake mt
30H1 Teshio-gawa r.
30J1 Teshio-sanchi mts
49B1 Tesouras r.
50C3 Tessaoua
13F7 Test r.
20C6 Testour
53D5 Tete
17P5 Teteriv r.
17O6 Tetiyiv
50B1 Tétouan
21J3 Tetovo
48D2 Teuco r.
14F5 Teviot r.
14F5 Teviotdale v.
37A7 Te Waewae Bay
35L4 Tewantin
41H5 Texarkana
40G5 Texas div.
41H6 Texas City
55G4 Teyateyaneng
22G3 Teykovo
22G3 Teza r.
27H4 Tezu
55H4 Thabana-Ntlenyana mt
55G4 Thaba Putsoa mt
55H4 Thaba-Tseka
55G3 Thabong
29C4 Thai Binh
26F3 Thai Desert des.
29C5 Thailand
29C5 Thailand, Gulf of
29C4 Thai Nguyên
20C7 Thala
55F2 Thamaga
13F6 Thame r.
13G6 Thames r.
13H6 Thames est.
29C5 Thanh Hoa
26E4 Thar Desert des.
21L4 Thasos i.
29B5 Thaton
29B5 Thayetmyo
16B4 The Hague
38H3 Thelon r.
19H5 Theniet El Had
46F5 Theodore Roosevelt r.
21K4 Thermaïkos Kolpos g.
21K4 Thessaloniki
13H5 Thet r.
13H5 Thetford
41M2 Thetford Mines
50A3 Thiès
52D4 Thika
27F6 Thiladhunmathee Atoll
27G4 Thimphu
18H2 Thionville
11L8 Thisted
21K5 Thiva
45H2 Thomasville
38J4 Thompson
40H4 Thompson r.
16C7 Thonon-les-Bains
12F3 Thornaby-on-Tees
13E6 Thornbury
12G4 Thorne
43C4 Thousand Oaks
21L4 Thrakiko Pelagos
35J7 Three Hummock I.
16C7 Thun
39K5 Thunder Bay
16F7 Thurn, Paß pass
14E2 Thurso r.
47K4 Tianguá
28D3 Tianjin
28C3 Tianshui
50C1 Tiaret
50B4 Tiassalé
49B4 Tibagi r.
51D4 Tibati
20E3 Tiber r.
51F1 Tiberias, Lake l.
51D2 Tibesti mts
44B3 Tiburón i.
16D7 Ticino r.
44G4 Ticul
50C2 Tidikelt, Plaine du
50A3 Tidjikja
27F2 Tien Shan mts
44E5 Tierra Blanca
48C8 Tierra del Fuego, Isla Grande de i.
19D3 Tiétar r.
19D2 Tiétar, Valle de v.
49C3 Tietê
49B3 Tietê r.
41K5 Tifton
21L3 Tigheciului, Dealurile h.
23D6 Tighina
46F2 Tigre r.
46C4 Tigre r.
26C3 Tigris r.
26C5 Tihāmah reg.
44A2 Tijuana
49C2 Tijuco r.
23G6 Tikhoretsk
22E3 Tikhvin
22E3 Tikhvinskaya Gryada ridge
26C3 Tikrīt
16B5 Tilburg
13H6 Tilbury
50C3 Tillabéri
42A1 Tillsonburg
21M6 Tilos i.
22K1 Timanskiy Kryazh ridge
37C6 Timaru
23F6 Timashevsk
43D3 Timber Mt mt
50B3 Timétrine reg.
50C2 Timimoun
21J2 Timişoara
39K5 Timmins
47K5 Timon
29E7 Timor i.
34F1 Timor Sea
50B2 Tindouf
49E1 Tinharé, Ilha de i.
29G5 Tinian i.
21L6 Tinos i.
50C2 Tinrhert, Plateau du plat.
42C2 Tioga r.
42C1 Tioughnioga r.
19H4 Tipasa
47J4 Tiracambu, Serra do h.
21H4 Tirana
23D6 Tiraspol
21M5 Tire
14B4 Tiree i.
27F5 Tiruchchirāppalli
19G5 Tissemsilt
46E7 Titicaca, Lago l.
20G2 Titov Drvar
41K6 Titusville
13D7 Tiverton
20E4 Tivoli
44G4 Tizimín
19J4 Tizi Ouzou
50B2 Tiznit
44E5 Tlaxcala
50B1 Tlemcen
55F2 Tlokweng
53E5 Toamasina
31F6 Toba
46F1 Tobago i.
43D1 Tobin, Mt mt
29C7 Toboali
24H4 Tobol r.
47J5 Tocantinópolis
47J4 Tocantins r.
49C1 Tocantinzinha r.
31G5 Tochigi
31G5 Tochio
48B2 Tocopilla
20E3 Todi
16D7 Todi mt
29E7 Togian, Kepulauan is
50C4 Togo
43D2 Toiyabe Range
30J2 Tokachi-gawa r.
31F6 Tōkai
31G5 Tōkamachi
28E4 Tokara-rettō is
33J2 Tokelau terr.
23E6 Tokmak
27F2 Tokmak
31F6 Tokoname
30J2 Tokoro-gawa r.
55H3 Tokoza
30C5 Tok-tō i.
30E6 Tokushima
30E7 Tokushima
30C6 Tokuyama
31G6 Tōkyō
31G6 Tōkyō
31G6 Tōkyō-wan b.
53E6 Tôlañaro
19D3 Toledo
49B4 Toledo
41K3 Toledo
19D3 Toledo, Montes de mts
53E6 Toliara
29E6 Tolitoli
20E1 Tolmezzo
44E5 Toluca
40B4 Tolumne r.
22J4 Tol'yatti
30H2 Tomakomai
33H3 Tomanivi mt
19B3 Tomar
17L5 Tomaszów Lubelski
17K5 Tomaszów Mazowiecki
41J5 Tombigbee r.
49D3 Tombos
50B3 Tombouctou
19E3 Tomelloso
29E7 Tomini, Teluk g.
20G3 Tomislavgrad
24K4 Tomsk
30J2 Tomuraushi-yama mt
23G6 Tomuzlovka r.
44F5 Tonalá
31F5 Tonami
46E4 Tonantins
13H6 Tonbridge
29E6 Tondano
13E6 Tone r.
31H6 Tone-gawa r.
33J4 Tonga
55J4 Tongaat
33J4 Tongatapu Group is
28C3 Tongchuan
28E2 Tongliao
28D3 Tongling
28E2 Tongyu
27F4 Tonk
29C5 Tônlé Sab l.
31H4 Tōno
11M7 Tønsberg
40D3 Tooele
36G3 Tooma r.
54F6 Toorberg mt
35L4 Toowoomba
41G4 Topeka
16J6 Topoľčany
10W4 Topozero, Oz. l.
21M5 Torbalı
26D3 Torbat-e-Heydarīyeh
26E3 Torbat-e Jām
16F5 Torgau
23H5 Torgun r.
19D2 Tormes r.
10S3 Torneälven r.
10Q2 Torneträsk l.
39M4 Torngat Mts
28F1 Torom r.
39L5 Toronto
43D5 Toro Pk mt
52D3 Tororo
13D7 Torquay
43C5 Torrance
19C2 Torre mt
20F4 Torre del Greco
19D1 Torrelavega